WELCOME

To The Wonderful World of "Do-It-Yourself"

You have just joined the growing number of men, women and children who enjoy the thrill of creating with their hands. And you know the value of a dollar. That's why you will be intrigued by the hundreds of easy-to-build, money-saving projects contained in these pages.

You say you're "all thumbs"? No problem. When Steve Ellingson, today the world's most widely syndicated do-it-yourself columnist, started building his own furniture some thirty years ago, he knew little more than how to saw a board and hammer a nail. But he learned. And as he was learning, more and more people saw his work, and asked him to build things for them. But Steve had a better idea. Why not create simple-to-follow patterns, like sewing patterns, that an absolute novice could trace onto wood? Why not add simple, step-by-step directions and photos?

So he did. Today, U-Bild (which he founded) uses 15 designers to create handsome pieces of furniture, clever toys, unique handicrafts... and then tell folks how to make these items.

Schools, 4-H clubs, Boy Scouts and Junior Achievement organizations use U-Bild patterns and plans as part of their youth development programs. Hospitals, industries, church groups, senior citizen clubs and military units are also among the ranks of satisfied U-Bilders.

So welcome to U-Bild's worldwide family of do-it-yourselfers! You are one of those who affirm the words of Charles Kettering, famous inventor. "Learn how to use your hands as well as your head. There is a kind of practical knowledge and good sense which can flow into the brain only through the use of the hands."

READ STEVE ELLINGSON'S POPULAR COLUMN IN YOUR LOCAL PAPER... NEW PROJECTS APPEAR REGULARLY.

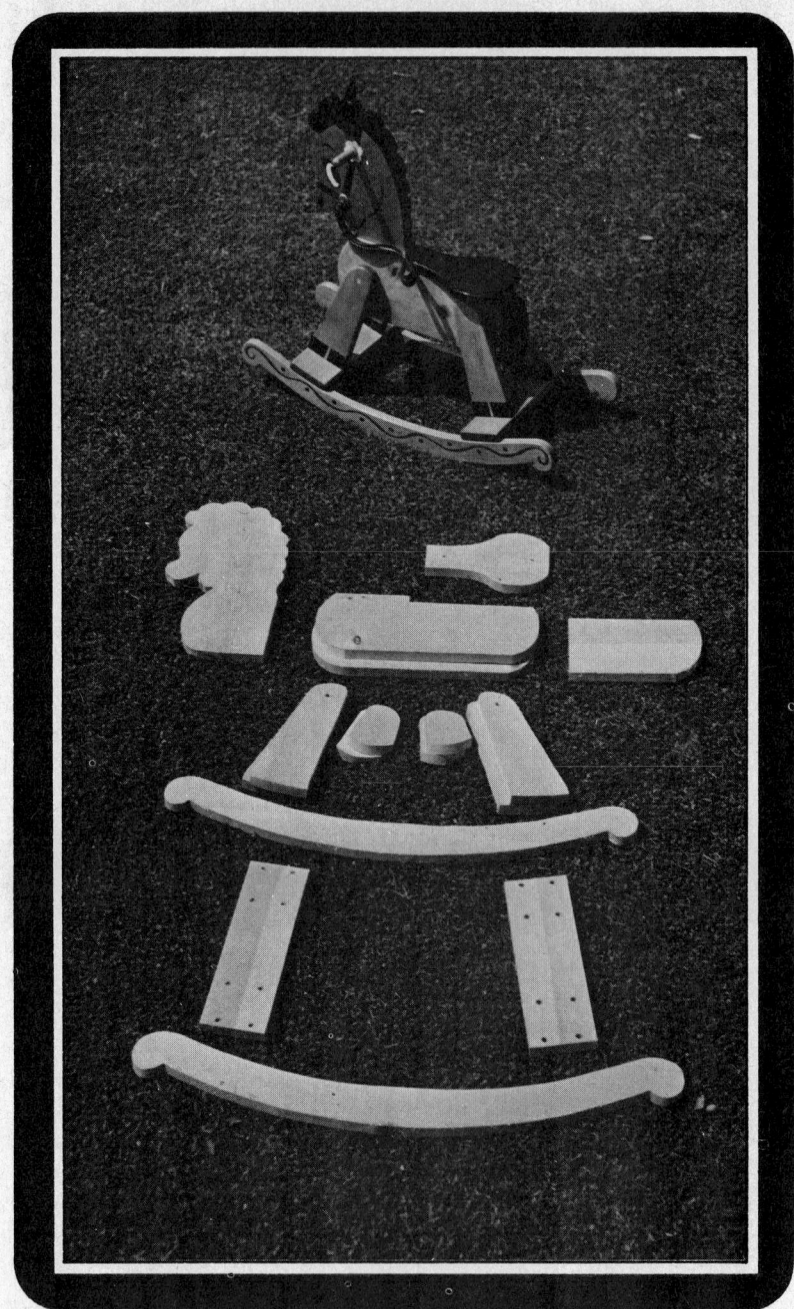

ALL U-BILD PLANS & PATTERNS FEATURE:
- Detailed step-by-step instructions
- Complete materials list
- Step-by-step photos, drawings and/or full-size traceable parts

"Copyright U-Bild Newspaper Syndicate, 1983. All rights reserved." Printed in USA.

READ ALL ABOUT IT!
Over 700 Easy-to-Do Projects

are pictured in the 112-page catalog, PATTERNS FOR BETTER LIVING. Now, with the help of Steve Ellingson's simple-step-by-step patterns and plans, you can create anything from a macrame wallhanging to a mountain cabin. Lawn furniture, interior furnishings, children's toys, recreational equipment, even handicrafts. You name it, there's a U-BILD PLAN that helps you build it yourself. To order, specify catalog in order blank below... only **$2.95** (includes postage)

HOT OFF THE PRESSES:

You'll enoy our popular 160-page CHILDREN'S TOYS & FURNITURE book, #FM7, containing step-by-step plans for 50 different projects .. **$7.95** (includes postage)

Pattern Prices are $3.00 unless Marked Otherwise

ASS POSTAGE & HANDLING

	1st Class
3.00	1.00
5.00	1.50
7.50	2.00
10.00	2.50

0 add: 25% for 1st class
esidents please
es tax.

n orders must **be accompanied by**

Oak Furniture Classics (#C55)

This classic collection includes three popular antique oak reproductions. The lawyer's bookcase is stackable... you choose whether it's 2, 3 or 4 shelves high. An oak file cabinet which will even hold legal-size hanging files. And the third member is the old favorite oak ice box. Retail Value — $9.00
Special — $5.75

TOTAL OF ORDER $ _____
LESS 10% DISCOUNT $ _____
(orders of $10 or more)
SUB-TOTAL $ _____
PLUS POSTAGE & HANDLING $ _____
(See chart)
TOTAL AMOUNT: $ _____

NAME _____
ADDRESS _____
CITY _____
STATE _____ ZIP _____

Please enclose check or money order for your pattern selection.

Place each pattern or book number in a box.

Check here for $2.95 U-Bild Catalog ☐

Box 2383
Van Nuys,
CA 91409-2383
BARGAINS, SEE INSIDE.

ORDER FORM
Some All-Time Favorites from our Catalog
(see inside for more exciting projects)

686 Oak Ice Box | **700** Lawyer's Bookcase | **724** Blanket Chest | **705** Oak File Cabinet | **727** 3-Drawer File Cabinet | **723** Single-Door Ice Box $2.00

456 Grist Mill | **239** Round Table | **713** Utility Building $3.00 | **318** Lawn Planter | **276** Glider Swing | **609** Window Greenhouse

62 BBQ Table | **213** Camp Kitchen | **352** Tree Seat | **642** Chopping Block | **597** Country Pine Sextet | **563** Sauna

 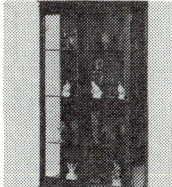    

672 Bookcase/Guncase | **709** China/Curio Cabinet | **657** Carousel Horse | **392** Child's Rocking Chair | **411** Dollhouse | **103** Child's Table & Chair

350 Outdoor Rocker  | **371** Wishing Well | **608** Sun Trellis | **C12** Birdhouses $4.00 | **694** Animated Windmill | **695** Farm-Style Windmill

All Pattern Prices are $3.00 Unless Marked Otherwise

FAVORITE HANDICRAFTS

- GM27 Flower Arranging $3.50
- H190 Egg Carton Flowers $3.75
- HH26 Cake Decorating for Beginners $3.75
- SP36 Nostalgic Crochet $3.75
- G464 Quilt Hoop Book $5.00
- G463 Fabric Ducks $5.00
- SP25 Traditional Quilting $3.75
- SP11 How To Sew A Quiet Boo $3.75
- J103 Crochet Favorites $4.00
- M801 Puffy People $2.50
- SP23 Kitchen Witch Faire $3.75
- L107 Horses & Unicorns $4.00
- U105 Drying Flowers With Household Products $2.50
- G470 Tiny Tots $5.00
- SP22 Soft Sculpture Dolls $3.75
- U104 Tole Painting Made Easy $2.50
- H229 Decorating With Collectibles $3.75
- G468 Pocket Teddy Bears $5.00
- U102 Zodiac Patterns $2.00
- GM43 Ribbon Frills & Fancies $3.50
- U106 Christmas Crafts & Wraps $2.50
- U110 Fabric Frames $3.50
- BL20 Blossom Children $5.00
- U103 Pine Cones: Gifts of Nature $2.50

ALL $3.00 EACH. PLEASE USE ORDER FORM & POSTAGE CHART ON REVERSE SIDE.

U-bild FAVORITE PROJECTS
SOME BRAND NEW!

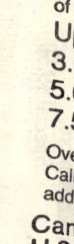

- 558 Grandfather Clock
- 530 School Clock
- 668 Bedframe & Headboard
- 632 Wooden Toys
- 56 Rocking Horse
- 363 Kiddy Kitchen
- 680 Chest-on-Chest
- 681 Silent Butler
- 682 Dump Truck
- 546 Toy Storage
- 614 Trestle Table
- 571 Rolltop Desk
- 612 Captain's Desk
- 478 Home Office
- 410 Jeep
- 662 Spinning Wheel
- 663 Mini-Rolltop Desk
- 667 Buffet Hutch
- 675 Wall Units
- 634 Antique Fire Engine
- 55 Lawn Chair
- 665 PVC Dining Set
- 461 Little Red Barn
- 288 Porch Swing
- 382 Pergola
- 174 Sequoia Chaise
- 649 PVC Lawn Set
- 603 Victorian Gazebo
- 678 PVC Lawn Swing
- 664 Water Wheel
- 348 Cupola
- 599 Spindle Cradle
- 628 Entertainment Center
- 579 Plant Furniture
- 658 Alpine Playhouse
- 397 Windmill
- 666 Heritage Cradle
- 648 Etagere/Wall Unit
- 572 Cedar Chest
- 671 Victorian Doll House

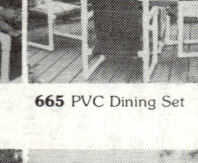

Handicraft Bonanza

LATEST PROJECTS ON PAGES 48-51

INDEX

AROUND THE HOME
Greenthumbing Needs
    Garden Caddy   7
    Greenhouses   4
    Greenhouse Mini-Plan   5
    Plant Care Books   7
    Planters   6, 7
Lawn Ornaments
    Flower Carts   7
    Grist Mill   8
    Tree Seat   14
    Trellis   7
    Water Wheel   8
    Whirligigs   8, 9
    Windmills   8
    Wishing Well   7
Lounging Furniture
    Chaise Lounges   10, 11, 12, 13, 14
    Lawn Chairs   10, 11, 12, 14
    PVC Furniture   12, 13
    Rockers   10
    Settees   10, 14
    Swings   11, 12, 13
    Lawn Swing Mini-Plan   18-19
Outdoor Dining
    Barbecue Tables   14, 15
    Outdoor Dining Tips   15
    Patio Galley   15
Patio & Home Improvements
    Brick Patio   15
    Carport   16
    Cupola   8
    Gazebos   7, 15
    Outdoor BBQ   14
    Patio Covers   9
    Patio Deck   9
    Spa Decking   9
    Waterfall-Fishpond   9
Storage
    Bike Rack   16
    Little Red Barn   16
    Patio Bench   16
    Pergola   17
    Tool Cabinets   17
    Utility Sheds   16, 17
    Workbench   17

INTERIOR FURNISHINGS
Beds & Bedroom Accessories
    Beds   28, 29, 30, 31
    Bunk Beds   29, 31
    Canopy Bed   30
    Cedar Chest   31
    Cradles   28, 29
    Cradle Mini-Plan   58
    Headboards   30, 31
    Hideaway Bed   30
    Infant Changing Table   29
    Portable Crib   28
    Wardrobes & Dressers   30, 31
    Waterbed Frame   31
Bookcases &
    Shelves   24, 25, 34, 35
    Bookcase Mini-Plan   39
Buffets & Cabinets
    Corner Cabinets   33

Country Pine Sextet   34
Curio Cabinet   34
Dry Sink   24
Kitchen Accessories   33
Sewing Cabinets   23
Stereo Cabinets   26, 27
Tea Cart   22
T.V. Cabinets   27
Clocks & Barometers   40, 41
Home Office Decor
    Captain's Desk   36
    Corner Desk   36
    Drafting Table   38
    Hall Tree   20
    Home Office   37
    Mini-Rolltop Desk   37
    Oak File Cabinet   25
    Rolltop Desk   36
    Secretary   37
    Standard Desk   37
    Trestle Desk Mini-Plan   42, 43
Wall Desk   37
Oak Ice Box   20
Plant Stand   38
Room Dividers   25
Room Remodeling   21
Spinning Wheel   47
Tables & Benches
    Benches   33, 34, 38
    Chopping Block   32
    Coffee Tables   22, 23
    Dining Tables   20, 33
    Hatch Cover Table   20
    Multi-Purpose Work Table   30
    Parquet Tables   22
    Silent Butler   22

HANDICRAFTS
Christmas Crafts & Wraps   46
Decorating with
    Collectibles   47
Drying Flowers with
    Household Products   46
Egg Carton Flowers   46
Fabric Frames   44
Fusing   47
Jeweled Ming Trees   46
Keepsake Hutch   44
Macrame   44, 47
Pine Cones: Gifts of Nature   46
Rag Dolls   45
Soft Sculpture Dolls   44
Stained Glass   44
String Art   47
Tole Painting   44
Quilting   45
Quiet Book   45
Weaving   47
Wooden Ornaments   45

KIDS & PETS
Children's Furniture
    Beds   28, 29, 30
    Giraffe Clothes Rack   60
    Rocker   59
    Rocker Mini-Plan   52-55
    Step Chair   59

    Table   59
Doll Houses & Furniture   62
Playhouses   63
Toys
    Airplane Swing   57
    Building Blocks   61
    Bulldozer   57
    Carousel Rocking Horse   59
    Dump Truck   56
    Firetruck   56
    Jeep   57
    Jungle Pin-Ups   61
    Kiddie Tractor   56
    Kitchen Set   59
    Kryon Star Flyer   56
    Panel Truck   57
    Pony Rocker   60
    Rocking Horse   60
    Slide (indoor)   61
    Tell-it Make-it Book   61
    Tractor/Trailer   57
    Wall Mural   61
    Wooden Toys   61
Toy Storage   59, 60
Cat Castle   60
Dog Houses   60

RECREATION
Bars, Bar Stools   64, 70
    Wine Cellar & Racks   70, 71
Boats
    Catamaran   65
    Deck Boat   65
    Knockabout   65
    Pram Dinghy   65
    Miniature Sailer   65
    Raft   65
Cabins   66
Camp Kitchens   68
Cartop Carrier   64
Exercise Equipment   68
Fishing & Gun Cabinets   67
Game Tables
    Card Tables   71
    Pool Tables   64, 71
    Table Soccer   71
    Table Tennis   68
Luggage Rack Mini-Plan   69
Sauna   64
Tool Caddy Mini-Plan   76

DO-IT-YOURSELF TIPS   72-82
BOOKS   83
GRAB BAGS   84
LATEST PROJECTS   48-51
THIS 'N THAT   85-110
(a potpourri of all-time favorites)
ORDER FORM   112

$3.00...All Pattern Prices are $3.00 Unless Marked Otherwise
(plus postage — see chart page 112)

AROUND THE HOME

A. Lean-To Greenhouse (#596)
Designed to attach to any wood, stucco, stone or brick house. Utilizes shatterproof fiberglass-reinforced plastic. Plan contains photos, drawings, and instructions. 12' long x 7' wide and 9' high.

B. Fiberglass Greenhouse (#573)
Built from simple post-and-beam construction. Can be adjusted to any size in four-foot increments. Plan includes a complete list of materials and easy-to-follow instructions. Grow vegetables as well as plants!

C. Window Greenhouse (#609)
Build on the wall of your house or fit it into your window. The depth is 12 inches, height and width are variable. Made with glass or plexiglass in a redwood frame. Full-size pattern and instructions.

D. Greenhouse (#557)
5' x 8' Gothic-style greenhouse features flow-thru ventilation. Made of polyethylene, it's shatterproof and inexpensive. Tools needed are a saber saw, drill and staple gun. Plan has step-by-step details.

U-bild

HOW TO BUILD A GOTHIC-STYLE GREENHOUSE
BY JOHN CAPOTOSTO

If you love growing things, whether vegetables for the family table or ornamental plants for pleasure, here's the perfect cradle for new life. You can give seedlings a headstart for outdoor planting or equip the greenhouse with relatively inexpensive heating and cooling devices to extend the growing season in even the coldest climes. Like people, greenhouses come in all shapes ... for instance the four different styles shown (left-facing page). To give you an idea of how easy these are to build, using step-by-step plans, here are a few excerpts from one I designed for U-Bild (#557). It's compact (5x8), yet allows the greenthumber plenty of headroom inside.

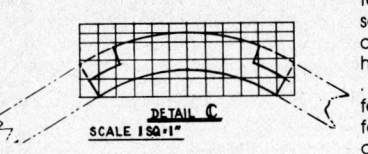

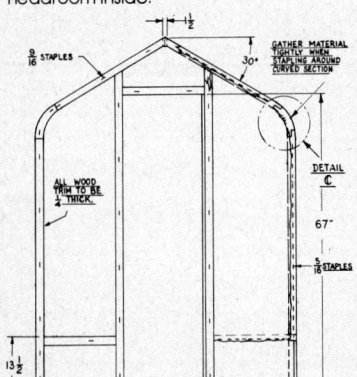

The key to the Gothic-style arch is Detail C. Using thin poster board and layout squares, transfer the design onto the board and cut out to create a template. Saw a 10 ft. length of 2x4 into 12" lengths. Trace the template design onto one length with a pencil and cut with a saber saw. Use this piece as a pattern to cut the other pieces.

Start construction with the base, cut from a 5/8" x 4' x 8' sheet of redwood siding. Cut seven strips 13-1/2" x 48" wide. Make studs (uprights) next, using 2x2 lumber cut from 2x4 stock. Have the lumber dealer rip these for you (eight feet long). Cut six studs to a length of 57-3/4 inches. Notch the bottom of each stud 5/8" deep x 13-1/2" long. Notch the top of each stud on the side opposite the bottom notch, 7/8" deep x 2" long. Cut four 57-3/4" corner studs. Notch the bottom on 2 adjoining sides, 5/8" deep x 13-1/2" long.

Attach the uprights to the base pieces at perfect right angles, using screws and waterproof glue. Add the curved sections next, then the rafters. With one side completed, add the ridge, screwing through the beam into the rafter ends with 2-1/2" screws. Use a temporary brace to support the assembly. Add front and rear framing next. Fasten rear base pieces to corner studs. Set the rear studs temporarily in place, centered on the edges of the base piece.

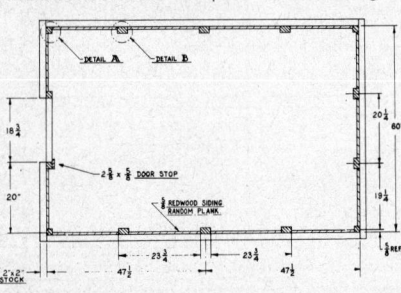

Cut the studs to required fit, notching each one at the bottom 5/8" deep and 13-1/2" long, then fasten to rafters and base pieces. Attach the head approximately 2" below the top of the studs.

The plastic sheeting used to cover the frame is available at most garden centers and comes in various sizes. Use material at least 4-mil thick and a good staple gun (I used a Swingline Powergun 1000). Cover the front and rear sections first. Cut the plastic slightly larger than required and staple them to the frame. Use 5/16-inch staples and space them about 3 inches apart. Pull the plastic taut as you staple. Trim excess plastic with a scissor.

The foregoing was just a quick synopsis of Plan #557, to give you an idea of how fast a job like this can go. The plan with its full list of required materials and more detailed procedure, right down to joint details A and B, enables even the greenest amateur (pardon the pun) to build this greenhouse.

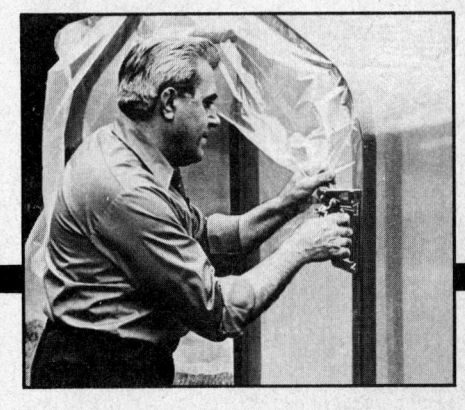

HOW DOES YOUR GARDEN GROW?

A. Redwood Planters (#562)
Make one or make them all. Detailed drawings and complete materials list included.

B. Victorian-Style Gazebo (#603)
To build, seat prefabricated dome on posts and fill in with lath. $2.50. Also available: #SD1 Gazebo Study Plan Book ... $7.00

C. Trellis Trio (#673)
Three different styles, each made from fir or pine with redwood stakes. 6' high.

D. Arbor-Trellis (#613)
Romantic walkthrough for any garden. Features full-size traceable arch pattern.

E. Floor & Hanging Planters (#283)
Made from scrap blocks of wood, these are a snap to build.

F. Garden Caddy (#285)
Goes where you go. Pegboard holds tools.

G. Wishing Well (#371)
Features redwood or cedar "bricks" for durability — wood or composition shingles add rustic touch. 6' high x 4' wide.

H. Lawn & Patio Planter (#318)
Features three stepped trays. 30" long x 20" wide x 32" high.

I. Deer Planter Trio (#745)
Build one or the whole family!

J. Planter Trio (#661)
A flower cart, "Red Flyer" wagon, and a wheelbarrow. Full-size traceable pattern.

O. Plant Furniture (#579)
Create them from cedar, fir or wood of your choice. Will fit any decor.

P. Donkey Cart Planter (#748)
Measures 41" long by 20" high and holds several different size flower pots.

A

B

D

F

G

O

H

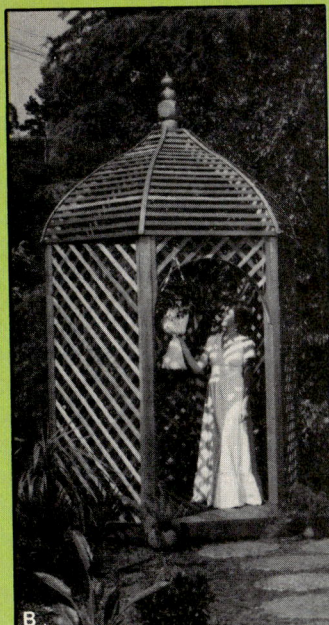

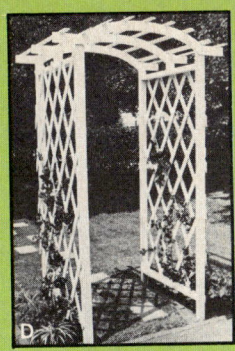

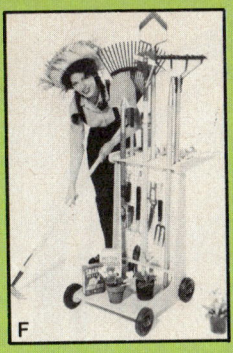

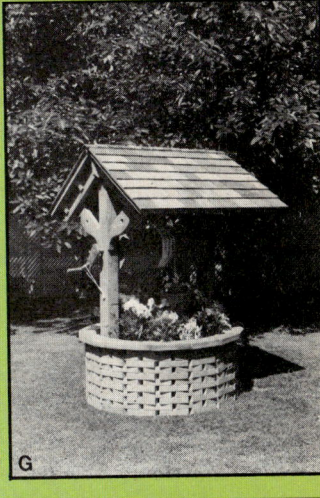

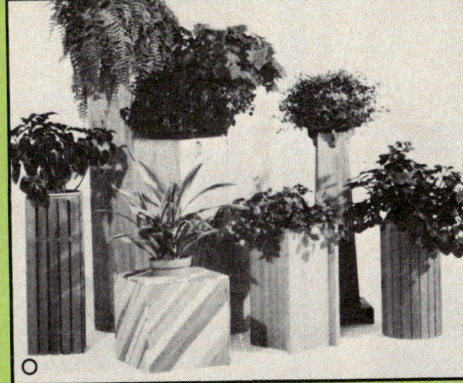

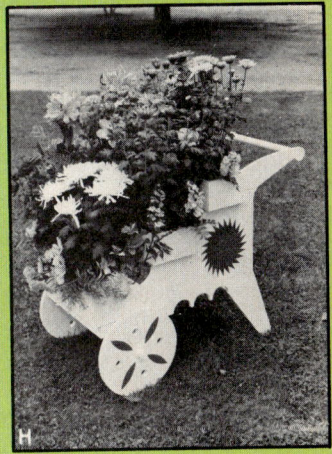

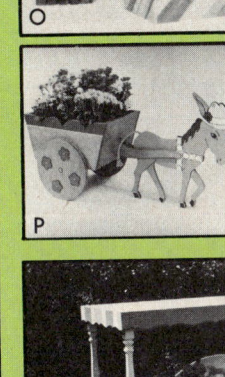

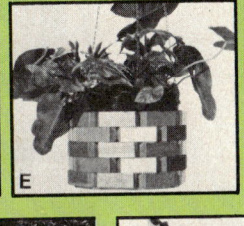

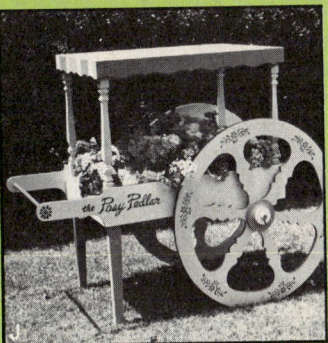

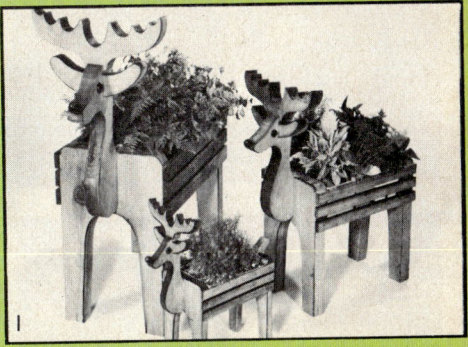

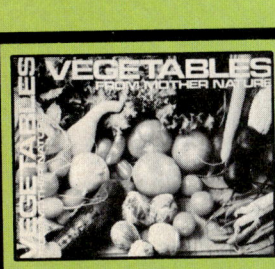

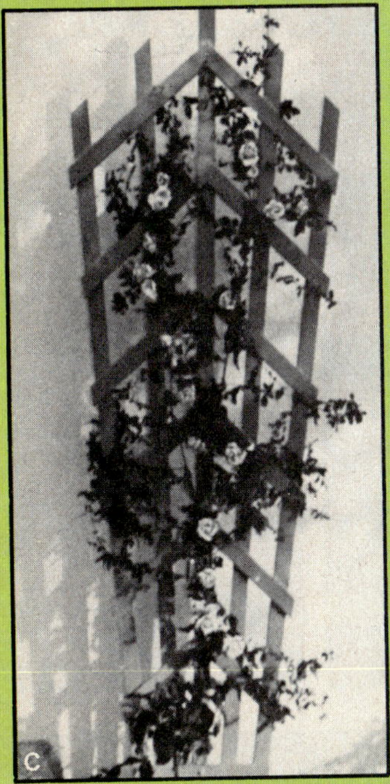
C

P

E

J

I

K. Vegetables from Mother Nature (#H801)
Color book helps YOUR garden grow. **$5.00**

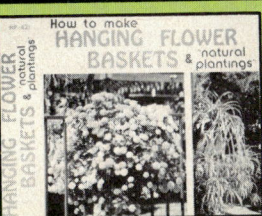

L. Hanging Flower Baskets (#H421)
33 pages of the latest in "natural plantings." **$2.50**

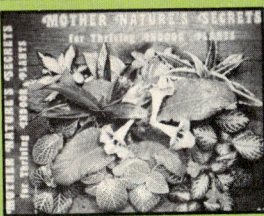

M. Mother Nature's Secrets (#H600)
65 pages about your indoor plants. **$4.00**

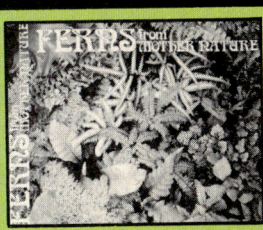

N. Ferns from Mother Nature (#H501)
Full-color Fern Album. 40-page book. **$3.50**

$3.00 . . . ALL PATTERN PRICES ARE $3.00 UNLESS OTHERWISE MARKED

(Plus postage – see chart on page 112)

A. Cupola (#348)
Ventilate the attic for a cooler house. Full-size pattern shows how to adjust to any roof pitch.

B. Grist Mill (#456)
Waterwheel turns by electric recirculating pump. Measures 48"l x 24"w x 50"h.

C. Dutch Windmill (#397)
Full-size pattern for popular lawn decoration. Measures 30"h, not including blades.

D. Animated Windmill (Whirligig) (#694)
Great ornamentation for flower garden or planter. Made from ¼" plywood and traceable patterns.

E. Farm-Style Windmill (#695)
Has 12 blades and a vane. Turns on ½" shaft with ball bearings.

F. Water Wheel (#664)
4' high, 3½' wide and 4' long. Drainage holes permit water to flow back to recirculating pump.

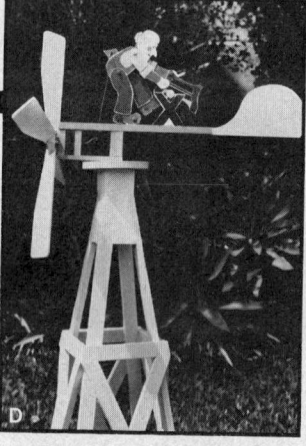

GET MORE RESALE $

A. How to Plumb & Deck a Spa (#670)
Step-by-step pictures and directions for installing a fiberglass spa... from digging a hole to line connections.

B. Wood Deck (#522)
Can be built from any weather-resistant wood in 4' x 4' modules. Drawings, materials list included.

C. Whirligig Duo (#730)
A colorful addition to your yard! Full-size traceable patterns make it a cinch. Each is approx. 24" long. **$3.50**

D. Sun-Trellis (#608)
This complete plan shows how to build a cover either 12' x 16' or 12' x 24' from cedar or Douglas Fir.

E. Waterfall-Pond Fountain (#508)
Measures 4' x 16' and holds 300 gallons of water. Step-by-step instructions and pictures guide you.

FUN IN THE SUN, ANYONE?

A. Double-Facing Chaise (Pattern #372)
Use with or without pads. Fits two standard 24" x 72" chaise pads and the adjustable back can be laid down flat for sun bathing.

B. Patio Rocker (#350)
Here's a sturdy, good looking and easy-to-build rocker made entirely of 3/4" plywood. Sides are one piece for strength and simple construction. Step-by-step plan also has materials list.

C. Double Rocking Recliner (#451)
Made of plywood and contoured to fit the body. Standard-size pads are used. Also available...
Single Rocking Recliner (#701)

D. Park-Style Bench (#712)
3 adults can relax comfortably on this bench which measures 30" high x 22" wide and 60" long. Full-size pattern includes traceable curves for the sides.

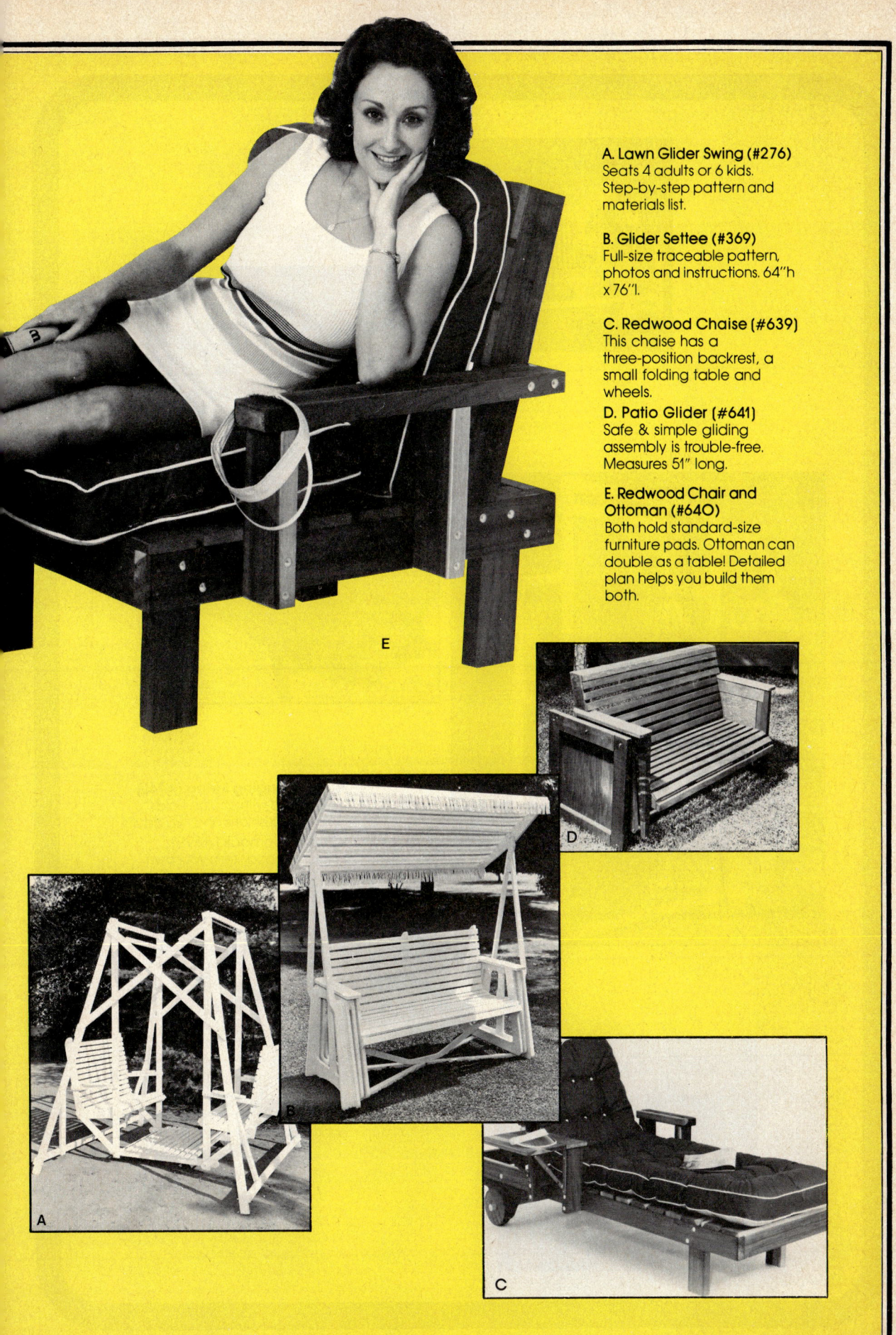

A. Lawn Glider Swing (#276)
Seats 4 adults or 6 kids. Step-by-step pattern and materials list.

B. Glider Settee (#369)
Full-size traceable pattern, photos and instructions. 64"h x 76"l.

C. Redwood Chaise (#639)
This chaise has a three-position backrest, a small folding table and wheels.

D. Patio Glider (#641)
Safe & simple gliding assembly is trouble-free. Measures 51" long.

E. Redwood Chair and Ottoman (#640)
Both hold standard-size furniture pads. Ottoman can double as a table! Detailed plan helps you build them both.

$3.00 ... ALL PATTERN PRICES ARE $3.00 UNLESS OTHERWISE MARKED
(Plus postage — see chart on page 112)

A. PVC Hanging Swing (#742)
Suspended with chains, holds standard cushions and two adults.

B. PVC Hammock (#699)
Enjoy the good life in your own backyard. Easy-to-follow directions and photos.

C. Sequoia Chaise (#174)
Adjustable back tilts or lays flat for sunning or "snoozing."

D. PVC Etagere (#702)
Its tempered glass shelves will hold plants, knick-knacks, books, etc.

E. Lawn Chair (#55)
Just trace the full-size pattern onto wood, saw it out and then assemble... fun and easy!

F. Hanging Swing (#288)
Hang this in your carport, patio, porch or branch of a tree.

A. Plastic Pipe Lawn Set
Use plastic (PVC) pipe to build chaise lounge, table, chair & ottoman (4 pcs.).

Plan #649
Full-size plan features diagrams and complete materials list.

B. PVC Dining Set (#665)
Make 4 chairs and 4' x 4' table from step-by-step directions. Use schedule 40 plastic pipe.

C. PVC Lawn Swing (#678)
Measures 4½' x 6' at the base and 6' high. It uses standard-size cushions. The canopy is removable.

A. Barbecue Dining Set (Pattern #62)
A sturdy table with two benches. Use on the patio or give it a more refined finish for inside use. 6' l x 36" w x 30" h.

B. Conestoga Wagon Settee (#315)
Features pull-out table for snacks and drinks. Patterned after original covered wagon. 8' long x 4' wide x 5' high.

C. Patio Lounger (#255)
Wheels make it easy to move or store away. The full-size pattern has lots of easy-to-follow photos and directions.

D. Tree Seat (#352)
Add interest to your yard with this easy-to-build slat seat. Pattern shows how to fit any tree.

E. Patio Chair (#291)
Make it with webbing or a standard-size chair pad. Can be painted or varnished.

F. Outdoor Barbecue (#162)
This concrete block barbecue is 74" long, 26" wide, and 5' high. The plan is fully illustrated and easy-to-follow.

A. Dining Set (Pattern #239)
Seats 8 or more, will support an umbrella. Wheels provide easy mobility of the table. 52" in diameter.

B. Teahouse (#710)
Measuring 7' x 7' the deck features built-in benches with a corner table. Follow step-by-step plans. **$3.00**

C. Brick Patio (#512)
Lay bricks with a sand or concrete base, with or without wood strips. Complete instruction sheet.

D. Folding Picnic Table & Bench (#732)
Table measures 6' long by 20" wide and seats eight. Pattern offers full-size traceable parts.

E. Table & Benches (#312)
This rugged table set seats eight and will last a lifetime. Pattern includes easy-to-follow instructions and materials list.

F. Redwood Picnic Set (#669)
This outdoor table can be made with the benches separate or attached. It measures 33" wide, but the length is optional ... 5' or 6' long.

G. Gazebo (#550)
Western-style garden shelter contains a firepit for outdoor cooking. 11' x 11' x 13' high.

H. Patio Galley (#342)
Great for parties! Sliding top becomes 5' long. Holds charcoal, towels and utensils.

SOME HANDY TIPS FOR OUTDOOR LIVING

1. Save those old egg cartons and put charcoal briquettes in them. Makes a convenient way to store them, and simple to light.
2. Keep a bucket of water next to your barbecue. After you've finished cooking, use some long tongs and pull out the coals and drop them in the water. Then dry them out and use them over and over.
3. To keep ants and mosquitoes at bay, cut up some old tin cans so that they are about an inch high. Fill them with oil of citronella and put each table leg inside one.

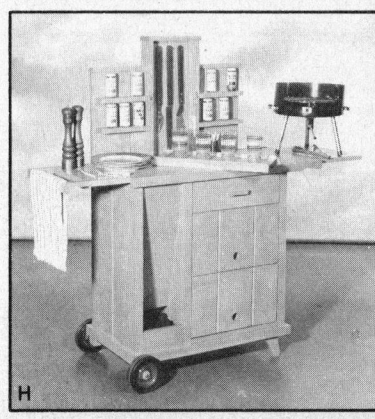

$3.00 ... ALL PATTERN PRICES ARE $3.00 UNLESS OTHERWISE MARKED
(Plus postage – see chart on page 112)

A. Little Red Barn (Pattern #461)
Here's a handsome storage shed for anything from garden tools to motorcycles. It measures 6' x 8' and can be enlarged in size easily. The pattern features step-by-step photos and instructions to guide you.

B. Pool & Storage Shed (#250)
A great place to store and lock your garden and carpenter tools. Also, it's perfect as a dressing room for the poolside. The children might even like it for a playhouse! Increase or decrease the size as necessary. 6'high x 4'wide x 4'long.

C. Car Port (#235)
Garages these days just aren't big enough, so here's a shelter for your car or boat, plus it's also a shady place to work outdoors. Meets all building code requirements and the step-by-step plan includes many handy tips.

D. Bike Rack (#419)
Strong enough to withstand outdoor use, this rack may be built to hold one or a dozen bicycles. Made of 3/4" exterior fir plywood, this project is simple enough for the kids to build!

E. Patio Storage Bench (#423)
It's a comfortable seat and a handy hideaway. Holds patio gear such as bags of charcoal, garden tools, furniture pads, etc. Measures 68" long by 30" wide by 36" high. Easy-to-build.

STOW IT!

A. Utility Building (Plan #713)
This 8'x8'x12' structure has a roomy interior with securable window and door. Step-by-step pictures from pouring the slab to shingling the roof.

B. Tool Cabinet (#316)
Attaches to wall, carport, or apartment house car-stall. When doors are open it spans 6' for hanging tools, but when closed it only protrudes 6". Fold-down workbench provides 9 sq. feet of space.

C. Space-Saver Wall Cabinet (#405)
Versatile wall cabinet requires little space but provides lots of storage room. It even holds a portable sewing machine or vacuum cleaner.

D. Workbench (#535)
It features an easy-glide drawer and sliding doors. Primarily built from plywood, it stands 32" high, 24" wide and 48" long.

E. Functional Pergola (#382)
Use for entertaining, gardening and storage. 23' x 12' x 10'. Step-by-step plan, photos and complete materials list.

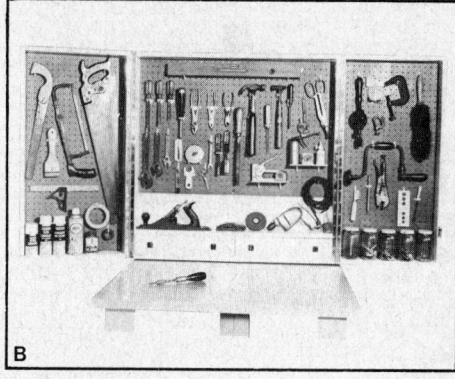
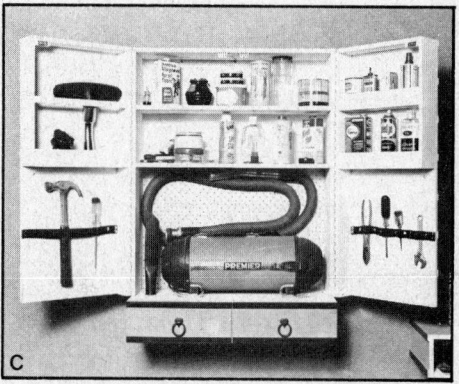
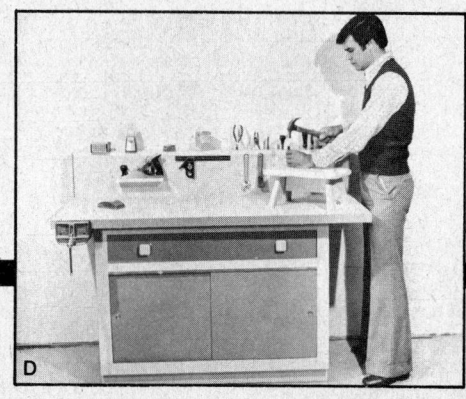

mini-plan

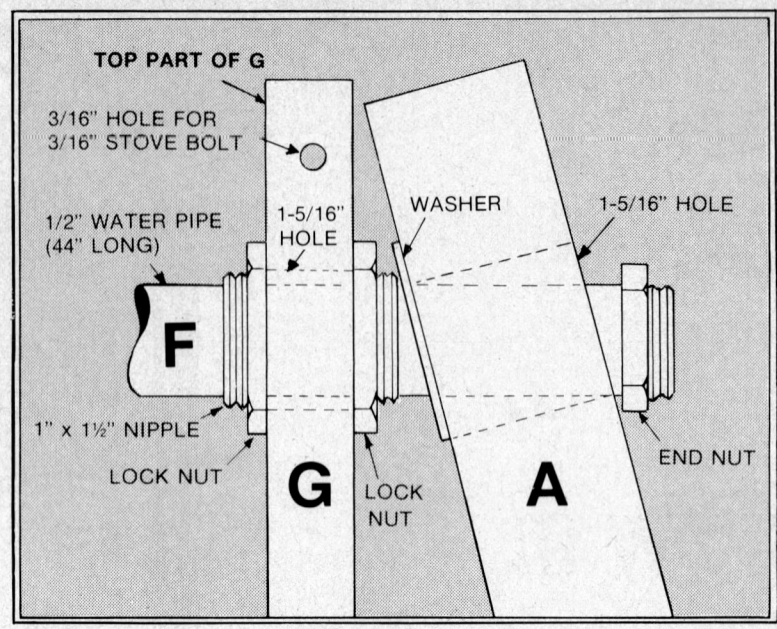

CONSTRUCTION DETAILS

The once-popular glider swing has almost vanished, like so many other good things of the past. Nothing was more conducive to relaxation, to neighborly conversation or pleasant entertaining on warm evenings outdoors. And, with their graceful lines and neatly painted coloring, few things added more to the graceful atmosphere of the home lawn.

Fortunately, the lawn swing has not been completely forgotten, and is now actually regaining its former popularity. This is a project that will prove completely engrossing to any handyman, and the result is a practical home accessory that can be used by the entire family for many years of pleasurable and satisfactory service.

The dimensions and assembly details are clearly indicated in the sketches. All parts are designated by code letters, so it is really easy to follow the assembly instructions by referring to the sketches as you progress with construction.

Cut out all the four A parts, each 7 ft. 10 in. long, from the 1-1/2 x 3-1/2-in. stock. These are the longest parts and form the basic yoke of the frame. Drill each of the A parts for the three 5/16-in. holes, and the one 1-5/16-in. hole, shown in Figure 4, locating the holes at the point indicated.

Arrange these parts on a flat surface in pairs, as indicated in Figure 1. Take the measurements carefully and cut out parts B and C to fit. Drill these parts and assemble to the A frame with bolts and screws. Axle F will help hold the parts together at the top. Next, cut the four D parts, and drill as indicated for three 5/16-in. holes. These D parts form the cross brace, which is bolted to the A parts in the upright position.

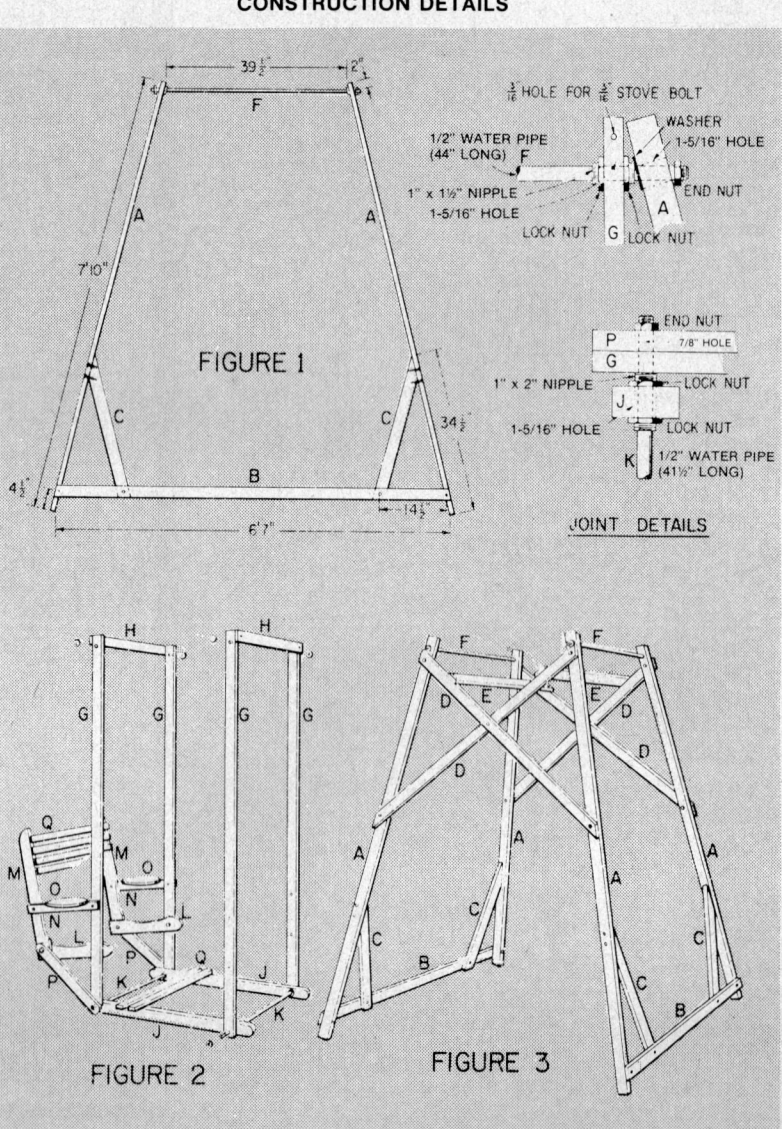

18

Measure and saw the E parts, and fasten across the D brace at the top with the number 10 x 1-1/2-in. screws. These E parts are located about 12 in. away from where the brace joins the A yoke. Saw the four 7-ft. 1-1/2-in. G parts and drill 1-5/16-in. hole in one end for the 1 x 1-1/2-in. pipe nipples. Press the nipples into the holes and lock in place with lock nuts. Hang one of the G parts in position by inserting axle F into the nipple, checking the swinging arc to be sure that it clears brace B.

Make two J parts as shown in Figure 4, each with two 1-5/16-in. holes, 36 in. apart. Put the 1 x 2-in. nipples through the holes and lock with nuts. The assembly for both the G and J parts is clearly shown in Figure 4 of the sketch. The distance between the two F axles is 36 in., the same as the distance between the 1-5/16-in. holes in part J, which means that the vertical G parts supporting the lower platform will be parallel.

Cut the H parts and assemble between the G members over the axle F, and complete the assembly of the platform by putting axle K through the nipples in parts G and J.

With the basic assembly completed, make the swing seats. Cut parts L, M, N, O, and P from the pattern by following the outlines in the ruled squares. Drill holes as specified, and assemble as shown in Figure 2.

Saw the required slats, Q, and nail in place, spacing the slats uniformly at all times. You might use a narrow strip of wood, about 1/2-in. wide, as a spacer guide, placing this strip next to each slat before the next one is nailed on. Three different lengths are needed for these slats. They are for the seat, back, and platform.

Counterset all nailheads. Paint all parts carefully, partly disassembling any joint where necessary to reach the wood underneath, so that your swing is well-protected against the elements.

NOTE: This is a mini-plan. If you wish to obtain our full-size plan with traceable parts, order #276

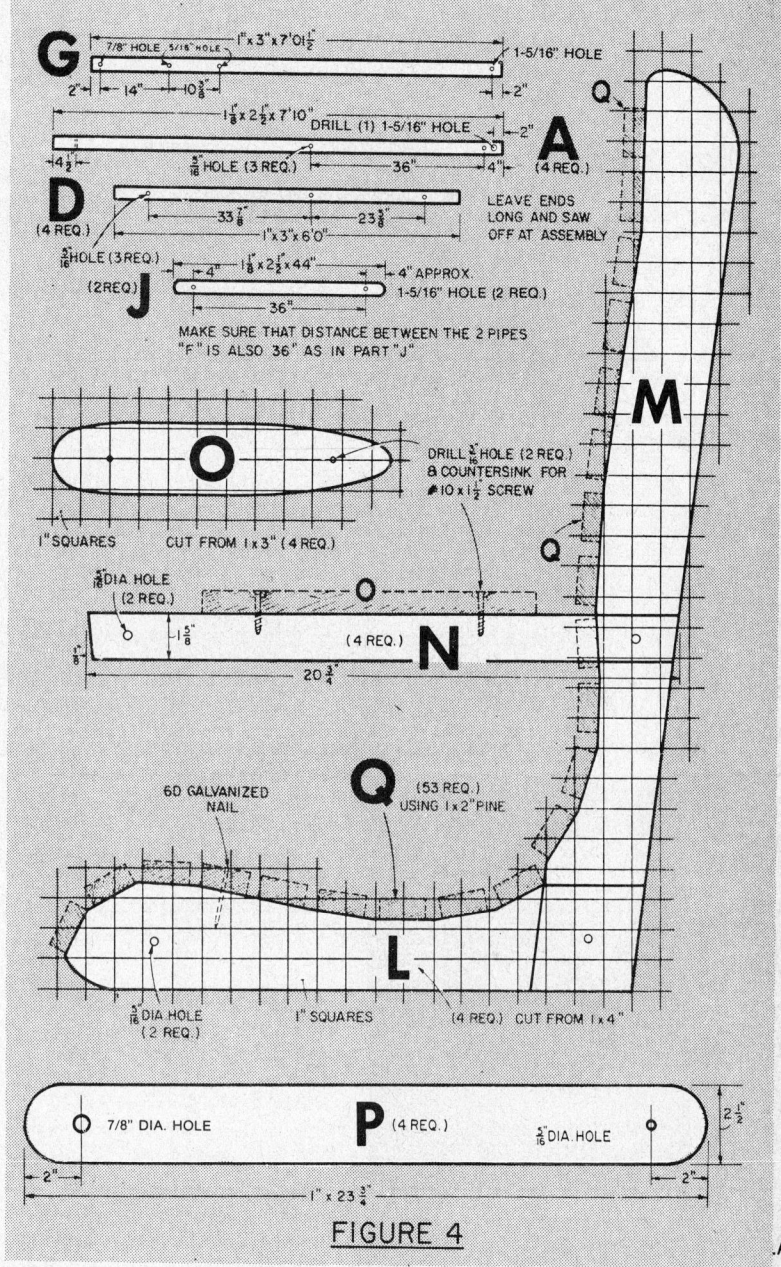

FIGURE 4

LAWN SWING MATERIALS LIST

The wood parts are given in their actual dimensions. Consult your lumber dealer to determine the type of wood stock that will permit you to obtain the thickness required, buying the material that comes closest to what is needed. For example, what is known as 5/4 lumber actually will be close to the 1" thickness in some cases, and 1-1/8" thickness in other stock.

No. Req.	Size and Description
5 pcs.	1-1/2" x 3-1/2" x 8' for parts A & J
2 pcs.	1-1/2" x 3-1/2" x 6' for parts C
9 pcs.	1" x 3" x 8' for parts B, E, G, P, H
5 pcs.	1" x 3" x 6' for parts D & O
1 pc.	1" x 4" x 8' for part L
2 pcs.	1" x 4" x 6' for parts M
28 pcs.	1" x 2" x 8' for parts N & Q
16	#10 x 1-1/2" flathead wood screws, for parts O & E
4	5/16" x 4-1/2" carriage bolts, with nuts and washers
16	5/16" x 2-1/2" carriage bolts with nuts and washers
14	5/16" x 2" carriage bolts with nuts and washers
4	3/16" x 3-1/2" stove bolts with nuts and washers
8	#12 x 2-1/2" flathead wood screws for parts C
	6d galvanized nails for parts Q
2 pcs.	water pipe 1/2" x 44" threaded both ends, with end nuts
2 pcs.	water pipe 1/2" x 41-1/2" threaded both ends, with end nuts
4	nipples 1" x 2" with 16 locking nuts
4	nipples 1" x 1-1/2" with 16 locking nuts
8	end nuts for 1/2" pipe
4	flat washers 7/8" I.D.

INTERIOR FURNISHINGS

A. Ice Box (#686)
An authentic-looking reproduction with ample storage for bar stock and accessories. Stands 38" high x 24" wide and 16" deep.

B. Hatch Cover Table (#598)
This nautical-style table is built from Douglas fir, so there is no need to obtain an actual hatch cover. 5 ft. long x 27"w. x 16"h.

C. Hall Tree (#592)
Build this from 2 x 2's and plywood. Seat opens to provide storage space. Pattern includes easy-to-follow directions.

D. Round Oak Table (#722)
Use our traceable pattern and ¾" oak plywood to build... then purchase chairs to match.

A. Bathroom Vanity (#624)
Dress up your bathroom. Build a 24", 36" or 48" cabinet.

B. How to Panel (Plan #569)
Step-by-step instructions on every phase of paneling. **$1.50**

C. Kitchen Cabinets (#721)
Four door styles 24" deep and 36" high. Width varies 18" to 48".

D. Advanced Kitchens (#FM4)
160-page source book of kitchen design ideas. Color photos and diagrams are included. **$6.95**

E. Best Baths (#FM1)
Plans and innovative ideas for remodeling or building a new bathroom. 160 pages. **$6.95**

F. Cabinets, Bookcases and Closets (#FM5)
32 different ideas for that additional storage. **$6.95**

G. Furniture Repair & Restoration (#FM2)
Instructions include stripping, repairing burns, dents, scratches, veneering, etc., 160 pages. **$6.95**

H. Garages & Carports (#FM3)
Build a new structure or add on to your existing home. **$6.95**

I. Energy Book (#647)
Handy guide for putting your house in shape, conservation-wise. 80 pgs. **$2.00**

$3.00 ... ALL PATTERN PRICES ARE $3.00 UNLESS OTHERWISE MARKED
(Plus postage – see chart on page 112)

"...YOU SAY YOU BUILT THIS?"

A. Tea Cart (#708)
This gracious serving cart was made from pine, but you can use the wood of your choice. With leaves folded it measures 28" high x 30" long x 16" wide. Step-by-step photos make it easy.

B. Parquet Tables (#685)
Made from wood parquet tiles used for flooring. Most are prefinished by the manufacturer. Tables measure 49½" l x 25½" w x 17" h and 25½" square x 19" h. An "easy-does-it" project.

C. Sofa Table (#752)
Fits easily behind your davenport. Made from oak tiles, it measures 54½" l x 13¼" w x 28" h.

D. Silent Butler (#681)
He can be your den coffee table or standing on his feet he'll hold your clothes for you. Just trace the full-size pattern, cut out and assemble.

E-F. Sewing Cabinet (#368)
The cabinet measures 36" long, 15" wide and 44" high. Three slide-out trays, pattern file, and drawers hold materials.

G-H. Folding Sewing Table (#385)
Fully extended it's 6' long x 20" wide – folds to 20" x 22". Holds any size portable machine and has lots of cutting area.

I. Multi-Purpose Table (#604)
36" x 48" – great for a sewing table. Built from pine or fir, it's sturdy and adjustable.

J. Fold-Out Sewing Cabinet (#454)
Arrange tools on backs of doors and materials in 8 drawers of assorted sizes. The top becomes a cutting table.

K. Coffee Table (#538)
This display case is tailor-made for coins, stamps, jewelry, etc. The glass top allows for easy clean-up after entertaining.

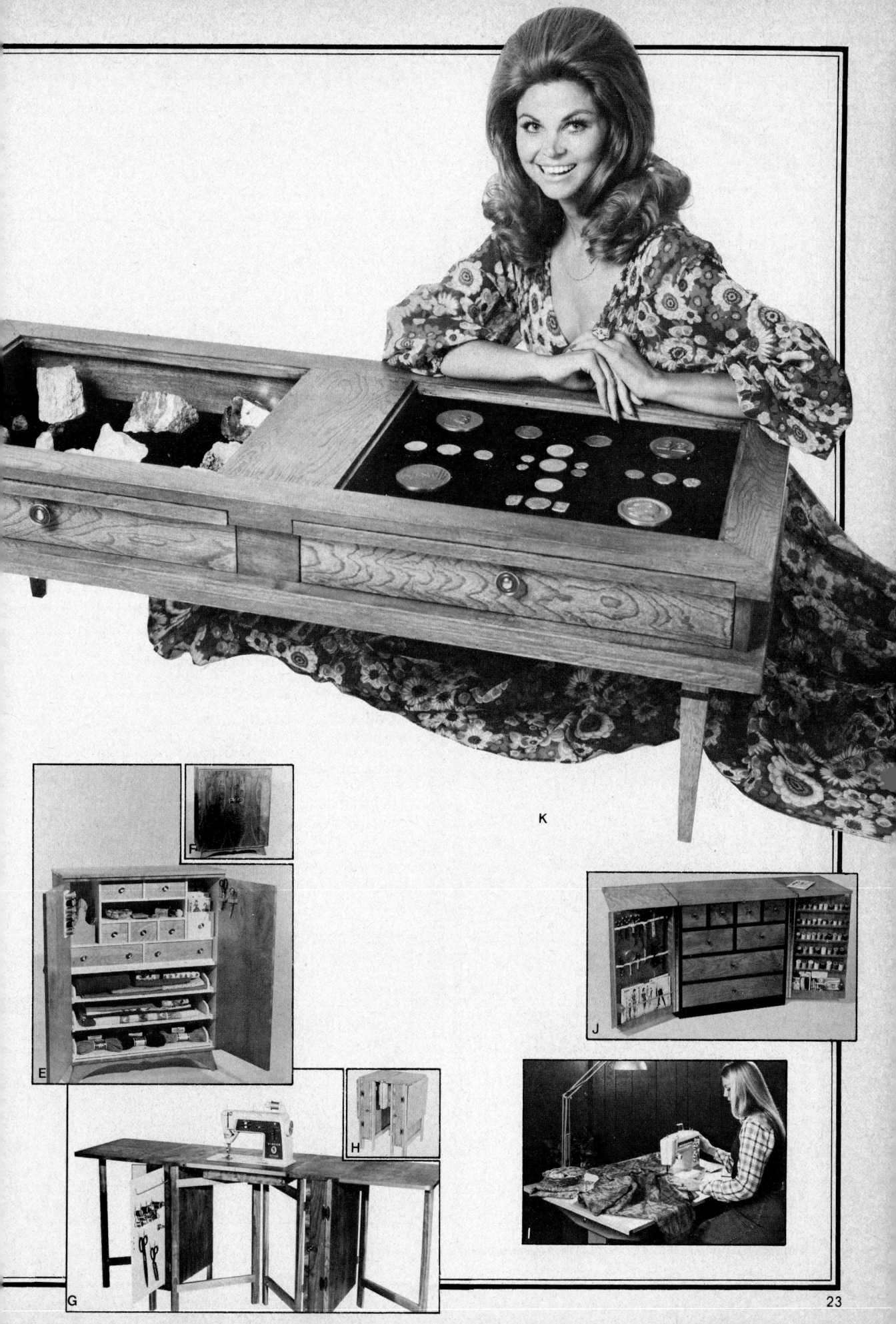

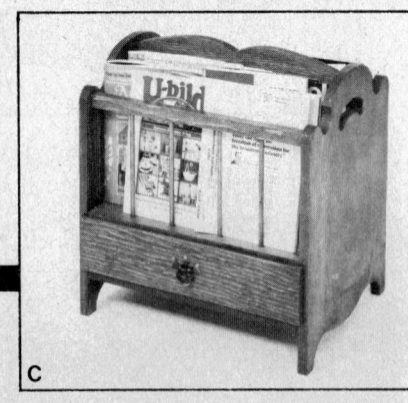

THE ORGANIZERS

A. Lawyer's Bookcase (Plan #700)
This antique reproduction is 5' high x 4' wide x 1' deep and is built in four units. Its glide-out glass doors tilt up and into the case on a dowel-pin guide system. Step-by-step pictures and instructions allow the amateur woodworker to build this one.

B. Magazine Rack (#377)
Here's a slim-profile rack which holds almost 60 magazines and can be placed just about anywhere ... it may even be hung on a wall. Casters provide easy mobility and shelf bottom is great for books. Full-size traceable pattern makes it a one-weekend project. 21" l x 8" w x 37" h.

C. Magazine Stand (#637)
This easy-to-build stand is made from pine lumber and doweling. It has four ample sections to hold all sizes of magazines and a bottom drawer to store miscellany. Just trace the full-size pattern onto wood, cut out and assemble.

D. Dry Sink (#307)
Easy-to-build version of American favorite has many modern uses. It's a great place to house speakers and components, for storing linens and silver, or can become a liquor cabinet. Adjustable shelves accommodate different size items.

A. Bookcase (Pattern #672)
Decorative wood mouldings and your choice of brass handles or knobs give this bookcase a professional look. Built from ash plywood and pine, its dimensions are 74" high, 33" wide and 17" deep. Glass panes can replace the wire mesh if desired.

B. Oak File Cabinet (#705)
This authentic-looking reproduction of an antique oak file cabinet measures 32" high x 19" wide x 21" deep. Holds regular and legal-size folders, and is adjustable to accommodate hanging file folders. **$2.75**

C. Caravan Room Divider (#515)
Here's a wall on wheels built on casters so you can swing it out as a room divider, or back it up against a wall. Houses music equipment or a TV, with pull-out typewriter or serving table option. Includes tips on choosing wood.

D. Etagere/Wall Unit (#648)
Contemporary in style, and versatile in function. You can build the smaller one alone as an etagere, or build them together for one wall unit. Shelves are fully-adjustable. Includes directions on making a desk, and a two-door cabinet.

$3.00 ... ALL PATTERN PRICES ARE $3.00 UNLESS OTHERWISE MARKED
(Plus postage – see chart on page 112)

LEND AN EAR!

As enthusiasm for sight and sound electronics equipment continues to grow, a new space in the home or apartment called the Home Entertainment Center is emerging. And with the four projects featured on these pages, it's never been easier to set yourself up with a unique center for sight and sound enjoyment.

First, determine how much space you have to work with. Then decide which of these four units will best suit your needs.

A. STEREO CABINET/WINE RACK. This unit features a slide-out platform for your turntable, space for your receiver, and room for built-in speakers on either side. When your system grows, and you want to move into larger unit space, this cabinet is easily converted (following our plan) to a handsome wine rack/bar. Pattern No. 645

B. TV/STEREO/BOOKCASE. This unit provides enough room for a complete Home Entertainment Center. A television, movie projector, video tape recorder, stereo components, tape and record storage are all allowed for in this roomy, handsome piece of furniture. Plan No. 628

C. RECORD CABINET/HUTCH. Built from standard pine, this unit gives you enough room for stereo components, plus tape and record storage. It will serve a double life as either a bookcase or china closet when your component needs change. Pattern No. 625

D. STEREO SPEAKER TABLE. Remote stereo speakers (either omni-directional, or small three-way speakers) are hidden in this beautiful table. Pattern No. 500

E. WALL UNITS. This TV/Stereo Center stores your tapes and records as well as doubling as a bookcase and desk. Made from 12 basic units either 16 x 16, 16 x 32, or 32 x 32. Arrangement shown is 9' wide x 6½' high. Plan No. 675.

Since there are an incredible number of options to choose from, and because sometimes the terminology sounds frightening, the following simple guide is designed to help you decide what's best for you.

RECEIVER: This is the heart of your component system. Basically, it is a box which can contain an AM/FM radio, pre-amplifier, amplifier and an assortment of knobs and switches that let you select the type of sound you want. The back sides of receivers generally contain several "jack holes" where you can plug in a turntable, tape deck or recorder. In choosing a receiver, you can buy amplifiers that have anywhere from 10 watts to 200 watts of power per channel. With 200 watts of power, you could probably be heard five city blocks away, so be sure you buy the right amount of power to match your needs.

TURNTABLE: Phonograph records are still the most popular source of music today, so you will probably want to purchase a turntable for your Home Entertainment Center. There are two basic types you will be considering – "manual" and "changer." The manual turntable lets you put on one record at a time, put the tone arm in place, and then return it to the arm rest. The "changer" allows you to stack more than one record at a time, then it automatically plays each one, and shuts itself off. For highest quality reproduction, as well as protection of records, most audiophiles prefer the manual turntable. The most important thing to look for is the tone arm. This arm contains a "cartridge" (which holds the stylus or needle) that picks up the signals from the record groove and translates them into electrical impulses for the receiver. The tone arm should be well-balanced, sturdy, and be simple to operate.

TAPE DECK: Basically, there are three kinds of tape decks to consider. Reel-to-reel, cassette, and eight-track. Reel-to-reel offers the best sound because of the 1/4 inch tape that it uses. However, the selection of music available in this format is more limited. For pure convenience, the eight-track and cassette formats are recommended.

SPEAKERS: The speaker is the "bottom line" of your system. Generally, you should plan on spending 1/4 of your component budget for speakers. The best location for speakers is at "ear level." When selecting speakers, play the type of music you enjoy listening to, and play it at the volume you generally enjoy. This will give you the best idea of how the speakers will sound in your home. When placing speakers, you can experiment with the locations that work best in your room. Remember that sound is constantly bouncing off of hard objects (like walls, furniture, etc.) and being absorbed by soft objects (rugs, drapes, etc.).

E

A

B

THE SANDMAN COMETH!

A. Rock-A-Bye Cradle (Pattern #300)
Simply trace the full-size pattern onto plywood, cut out and assemble. A standard-size mattress will fit.

B. Portable Crib (#689)
Perfect for families on the go! Strong, yet compact, it folds to 6" x 38" x 36" and uses a 18" x 36" mattress.

C. Speedboat Bed (#574)
Made from plywood and lumber, 'boat bed' measures 50" beam to beam and 96" stem to stern.

D. Country-Style Cradle (#599)
Measures 41" long, 18" wide. Full-size pattern utilizes pre-cut spindles.

E. Cable Car Bed (#507)
Modeled after the famous San Francisco cable cars, this 6' high by 7' long bunk holds standard twin-sized mattresses.

F. Twin Bed/Bunk Bed (#650)
This rustic bedroom set can be built from Douglas fir. Use as twin beds, or combined for a bunk arrangement.

G. Rocking Cradle (#644)
Inspired by colonial versions which let the mother knit or mend and rock the baby at the same time. Measures 51"l. x 17"w.

H. Bedmobile (#502)
A standard 39" twin mattress will fit this simple-to-build bed. Traceable pattern plus complete materials list.

I. Fire Engine Bed (#655)
Every kid wants to be a fireman and now you can help fulfill this ageless dream. Bed is built from plywood. Traceable parts.

J. Heritage Cradle (#666)
Balanced against tipping, it rocks with a touch of a toe. 28" high x 17" wide x 31" long.

K. Infant Changing Table (#690)
Measuring 36" long by 18" wide, its working level is 31" off the floor. Sturdily built from hardwood.

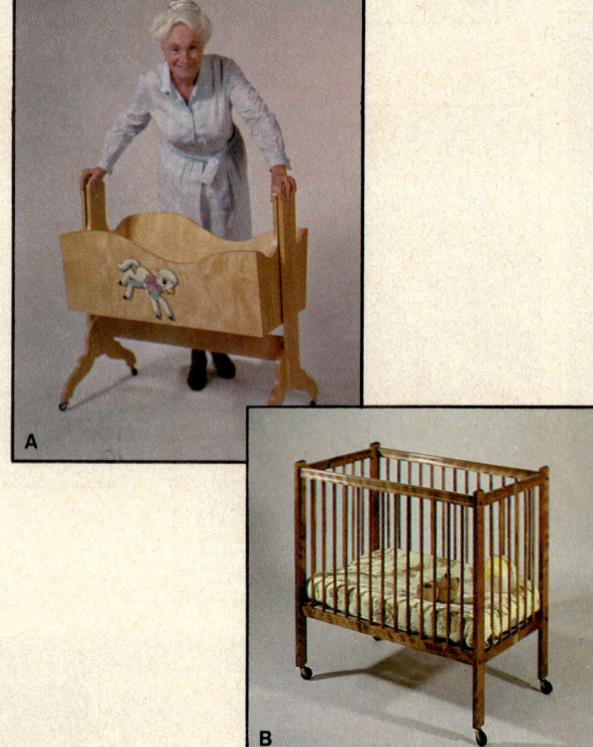

$3.00 ... ALL PATTERN PRICES ARE $3.00 UNLESS OTHERWISE MARKED
(Plus postage – see chart on page 112)

A. Bedroom Console (Pattern #653)
Headboard can be made to fit any size bed. Design allows you to use "track lighting" for reading purposes. Easy-to-follow directions.

B. Wallbed Unit (#494)
Requiring only the space of a twin bed, this unit offers 4 large drawers and the shelves hold a good amount of books and knick-knacks. Also on casters.

C. Dresser & Mirror (#691)
Dresser with matching mirror measures 54" wide by 33" high by 20" deep. Use pine or oak. Part of matching suite (see next page).

D. Canopy Bed (#581)
Full-size traceable pattern makes this an easy project. Holds a standard twin-size mattress. Uses pre-cut spindles.

E. Hideaway Bed (#707)
Convert any room to a guest room with this full-size bed which hides behind wall paneling. Bed is easily lowered and raised with the assistance of two springs.

A. Chest-On-Chest (Plan #680)
Traceable parts make it easy to build. Has shelves, 2 pull-out trays and 3 drawers. Measures 69" high x 41" wide x 20" deep. Part of 5-piece matching bedroom suite (#680, #691, #692).

B. Waterbed Frame/Headboard (#668)
Step-by-step plan includes material lists for Super Single, Queen, and King-size versions. We guide you in building the pedestal and platform . . . you buy the mattress, liner and heater.

C. Newport Bunk Beds (#323)
Has seven roomy drawers and a fold-down desk. Bunks are mounted on casters for easy gliding. Made of pre-finished plywood with easy-to-follow directions.

D. Cedar Chest (#572)
Measuring 48" long, 20" high and 19½" deep, this chest features a lift-out tray for storing small items. The plan even offers variations should you decide to use a wood other than cedar. Step-by-step directions and photos help you.

E. Nightstand & Headboard (#692)
The headboard can be made in three standard sizes, and the nightstand measures 22" wide x 20" high x 16" deep. Make all five pieces for an heirloom-quality suite (see #691 & #680).

BON APPETIT!

A. Chopping Block (Pattern #642)
Four square feet of work space with its own knife holder. Build out of pine, Douglas fir, or maple – simple step-by-step photos and instructions show you how.

B. Corner China Cabinet (#659)
This glass-enclosed china cabinet is made from pine and accented with brass hardware. Step-by-step instructions, pictures and materials list are inlcuded.

C. Swing-Up Wall Table (#173)
Use as a work table, for dining, a writing desk, etc. When not in use, swing it up against the wall.

D. China/Curio Cabinet (#709)
Measuring 72" x 35" x 15" it can be made with any wood of your choice. Features glass shelves and a fluorescent fixture.

E. Trestle Table (#614) & Bench (#615)
Country-styled furniture you can build from traceable pattern parts. The table is 7' x 33' and stands 28" high. Build the bench for casual dining or buy spindle-back chairs.

F. Breakfront China Cabinet (#667)
6' tall and 3' wide with serving area, storage, and magnetic-catch glass doors.

G. Welsh Cabinet (#141)
Measures 55" high by 27" wide. Has ample drawer, shelf and storage space.

H-I. Folding Table (#334)
Pulls out to 8' and seats 10, or folds to a 16" buffet. Easy-to-build.

J. Kitchen Cupboard & Stepstool (#703)
Curio Cupboard measures 6' high. Includes design for wheat motif which can be carved or routed.

K-L. Kitchen Quartet (#633)
Patterns for knife rack, board, wine rack, planter. Step-by-step pictures.

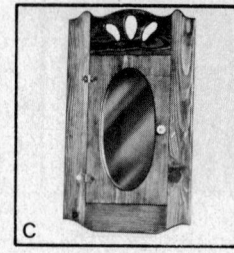
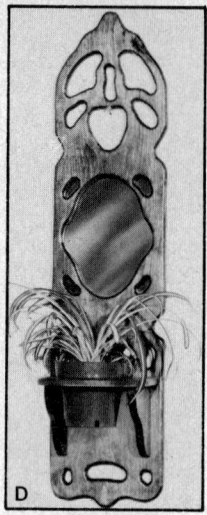

A-D. Country Pine (#597)
Step-by-step directions and exploded drawings for box, phone cover, bread box, towel rack, planter plaque & medicine cabinet.

E. Pocket Book Gallery (#391)
This project can be made from scrap plywood. Holds knick-knacks as well as paperbacks. The two drawers are handy for numerous odds and ends.

F. Cobbler's Bench (#60)
Add Early American warmth to your room with this bench/coffee table. Just trace the full-sized pattern onto wood, saw out and assemble. A cinch to make!

G. Curio Cabinet (#646)
This handsome unit stands over 6' high and features glass shelves and door. Easy-to-follow pattern includes many photos.

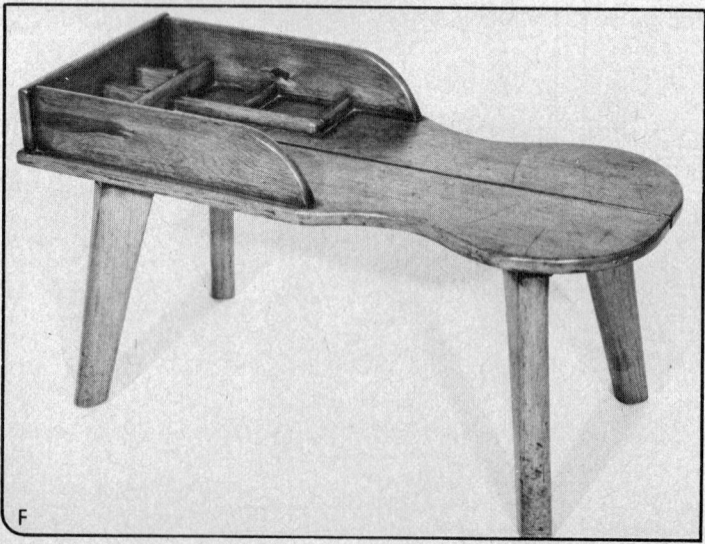

H. Growlight Bookcase (#652)
Perfect for African Violets and all indoor plants. Holds plenty of books. **African Violets Book (#H505) $3.50**

I. Wall Shelf (#432)
Compartments give 8 display sections for mini-treasures. 38" long x 24" high.

J. Corner Shelf (#267)
Made from scrap wood, this shelf provides perfect display space for mementoes.

K. Spoon Rack (#112)
Spoon racks make interesting conversational pieces and fit any space. Easy-to-build.

L. Collector's Shelf (#638)
Measures 31" high x 19" wide and has two drawers for storing odds and ends.

M. Wall Shelf (#328)
Built from plywood. 40" long x 20" high x 6" deep. Pattern includes step-by-step photos.

$3.00 ... ALL PATTERN PRICES ARE $3.00 UNLESS OTHERWISE MARKED
(Plus postage – see chart on page 112)

A. Roll-Top Desk (Plan #571)
This classic pigeon-hole style desk features 7 drawers, plus nooks and crannies for pens, papers, books, etc. Build from pine, oak or other wood. It has a look of timeless elegance that will make it a priceless family heirloom. Features tambour-strip cover. 43" high, 50" wide and 28" deep. Step-by-step plan is easy to follow.

B. Captain's Desk (#612)
Allows a maximum of writing space and minimum of floor space.

C. Corner Desk (#693)
Fits flush against corner walls. 39" high, 34" wide, 17" deep.

A. Mini-Rolltop Desk (#663)
A smaller version of a popular-style desk, built from oak or pine. Has 3 storage nooks and 4 roomy drawers. Stands 42" high x 35" wide x 19" deep.

B. Secretary/Desk (#683)
Build the top or bottom separately or bolt them together. Has a pull-down desk lid, 3 large, 2 medium, and 2 small drawers. The complete piece measures 80" h x 18" d x 32" w. **$2.50.** Also available, the guide for making leaded glass doors, #U108, **$1.50.**

C. Home Office (#478)
With doors swung open it measures 56" across. Will hold a typewriter, books, files, and papers.

D. Office-Style Desk (#286)
A professional-looking piece designed to harmonize with all types of interior furnishings. 60" x 29" top may be changed to suit you.

E. Wall Desk (#676)
Features a pull-down writing area, chalkboard, and 3 cubbyholes.

F. Trestle Desk (#435)
Traditional design with eight drawers for files and supplies.

A. Wood-Sculpture Plant Stand (Pattern #553)
Built from just one sheet of 4' x 8' lumber-core plywood, it fits in any problem corner. Use the four shelves for plants or knickknacks. Wood can be lacquered or hand-rubbed for rich tones.

B. Multi-Purpose Work Table (#604)
Step-by-step plan guides you in building this heavy-duty table measuring 36" x 48". Adjusts to three different positions. Built from pine, fir or construction-grade scrap lumber the frame is connected with stove bolts and wing nuts.

C. Colonial Bench (#279)
This bench also doubles as a table! Perfect for entry hall, dining room, living room or beside the fireplace. Step-by-step illustrations make it easy to build.

D. Deacon's Bench (#302)
An authentic reproduction of those handed down by our colonial ancestors. It measures 42" long by 24" wide by 38" high. Step-by-step pattern and materials list makes this one a cinch to build.

U-bild mini-plan

Nothing will encourage the use of a dictionary more than to have it handy. As a matter of fact, most reference books by their very nature are cumbersome, be they dictionaries, encyclopedias or a large family bible. Their value cannot be challenged and in any alert and progressive-minded household they are used continuously. Frequently, however, there is no suitable place to keep these books, particularly the one universal volume of continuous use—the dictionary.

The glide-about lectern bookcase shown here has a number of advantages for home, school or office. It's not only good-looking, but a practical library on wheels. You need only roll it up to your desk or study table to have all reference books conveniently at hand. The top tilts as shown, or it may be lowered to make a table. It's just the right height to be used as a lectern for speech-makers.

To order full-size pattern, see coupon on last page. Specify No. 376.

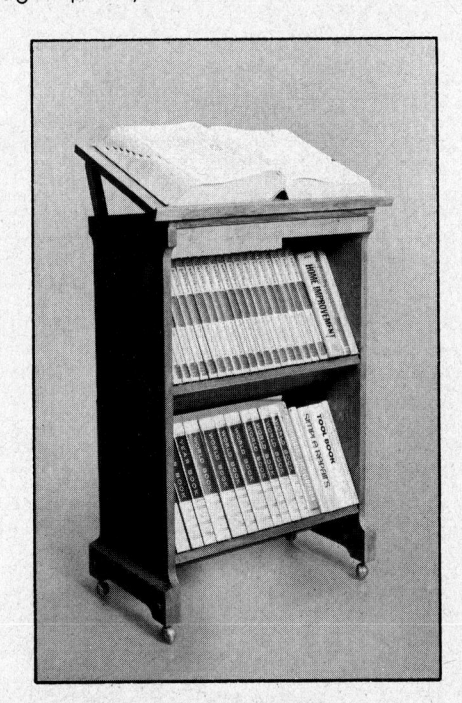

LECTERN/BOOKCASE MATERIALS LIST

No. Req.	Size and Description
1 panel	Selected 3/4" birch veneer plywood, 4' x 4' size
4 rolls	matching wood veneer strips for edgings
1 pc.	1/2" maple dowel, 3' long
1 pc.	3/8" x 1-1/4" birch doorstop molding
4	1/2" screwhole plugs
1	1-1/4" x 20" piano hinge and screws
2	corner braces and screws
4	No. 6/1-1/4" flathead wood srews (for attaching trim)
2	No. 8/1-1/4" ovalhead screws (for attaching Parts B)
2	dome-faced trim washers
2	flat washers, to fit No. 8 screws
	3d, 5d, and 6d finishing nails
	Glue, sandpaper, cement and wood filler
1 set	1-1/2" casters

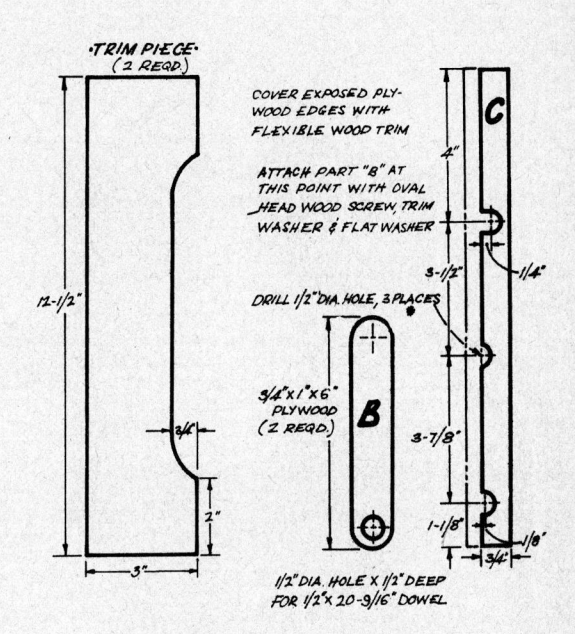

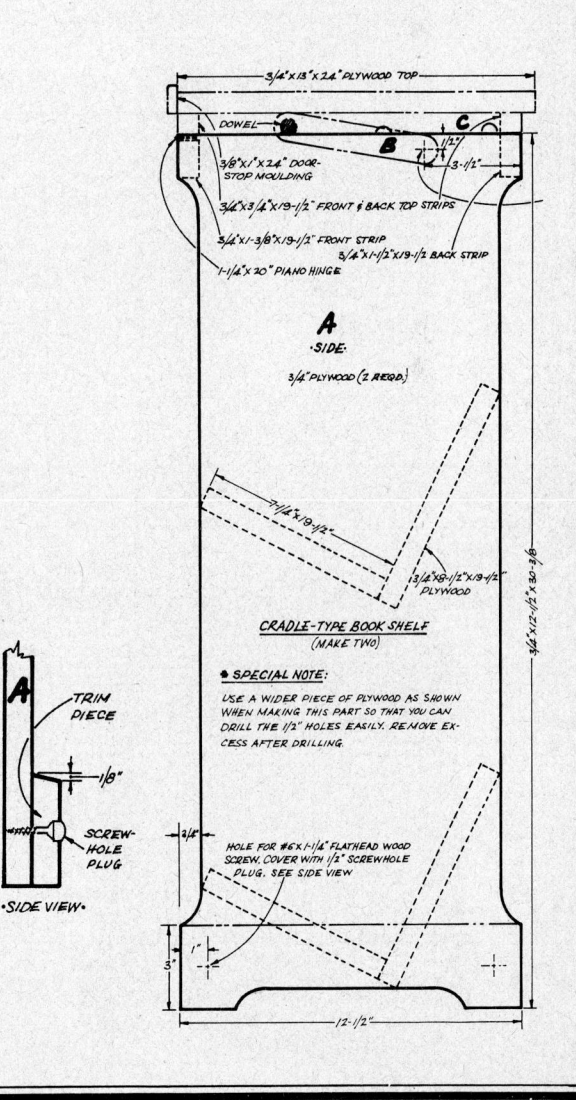

TIME ON YOUR HANDS?

A. Hall Clock (Pattern #464)
Stands just over 6 feet high and uses either weight-driven or battery movement.

B. Pendulum Wall Clock (#488)
Can be built in a couple of evenings with a few basic tools. Step-by-step pattern.

C. School Clock (#530)
8-side frame cut from one piece of pine. Movement uses standard batteries.

D. Barometer (#484)
3-dial instrument gives the humidity, temperature, and weather. Simple-to-build.

E. Wall Clock (#436)
Battery powered and can be hung anywhere. Just trace the full-size pattern onto wood.

F. Heirloom Grandfather Clock (#558)
Stands 74" high and uses the famous Westminster movement. Step-by-step pattern with materials list and photos guides you.

G. Granddaughter Clock (#485)
Colonial in motif, it strikes on the half hour and the hour. Approx. 5 ft. high.

H. Banjo Clock (#582)
A handsome addition to any decor. Measures 29" long x 9" wide and the pattern includes easy-to-follow instructions.

I. Grandmother Clock (#320)
A treasure to pass down from generation to generation. Includes step-by-step directions, illustrations and materials list.

J. Calendar Clock (#704)
Top dial shows the time of day... bottom dial shows month and date. Operates by an 8-day key wind Westminster movement.

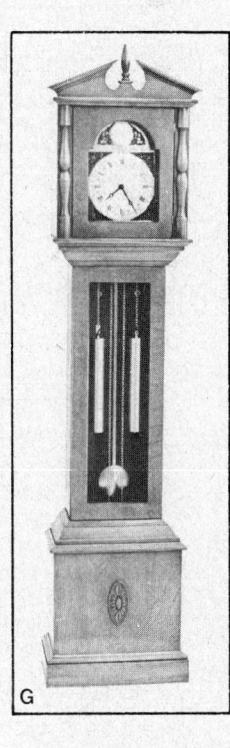

U-bild mini-plan

Here's a good-looking desk that you'll be proud to say you built with your own hands. It fits in with most furniture styles, is as suited for mom and dad as a "home office" as it is for the children as a study center.

The trestle desk shown here takes up a minimum of floor space, but still offers plenty of writing surface, plus eight drawers for files and supplies. Here is something that Dad will appreciate when he brings paper work home from the office. And, of course, report cards get a helping hand when the student in your family has his very own desk.

If you use the mini-plan (Figure A), trace the pattern onto heavy paper on which 1" and 2" grid squares are drawn. You can simplify this by ripping a strip of wood, about 26" long, to a 2" width. This makes it easy to locate guide lines for the squares.

When the squares are completed, outline the contours for the various parts, as shown, to obtain a full-size pattern. The same procedure is followed for parts calling for 1" squares on the plan.

Note that each leg is made of two pieces of 1/2" birch plywood glued together to form a single 1" thick leg. This means you must cut out four pieces to plan size and contour to make the two legs.

The two foot pieces are formed in the same manner, except that 3/4" thick birch plywood is used instead of 1/2" stock. Note that 1/2"x8" recesses are cut in each piece, making a 1"x8" slot when the foot pieces are glued together. The slot is to permit the recessed bottoms of the legs to be inserted into the foot pieces for assembly. Cover all exposed plywood edges of the legs and feet with matching flexible wood trim.

Having inserted the legs in the foot pieces (glue them together later), the next step is to make the cleats that are positioned at the top of each leg on the inside surface (see plan). These two cleats are made of 15" lengths of 1"x1" scrapwood with the ends shaped to the top contour of the leg pieces. They are attached to the legs with glue and No. 8x1-1/2" flathead wood screws.

Triangular-shaped 6" cleats (scrapwood) are centered and attached in the same manner to the inner side of each leg at points 5" above the floor line. These serve as supports for the contoured lower brace. All heads of screws should be covered with screwhole plugs, as illustrated. The exposed plywood edges should be covered with the flexible wood trim to enhance appearance, as in the case of the legs and feet.

After the upper brace has been put in place and attached to the cleats at the top of each leg, it is time to attach the desk base. This is cut to plan size (23-1/2"x42") from 3/4" fir plywood and attached to the square cleats and the upper brace part with glue and No. 8x 1-1/2" flathead wood screws.

Two dividers made from 3/4" birch plywood and cut to 3-3/4"x23-1/2" size are attached to the desk base with glue and No. 8x1-1/2" flathead wood screws at the points indicated on the plans. These are part of the lower drawers assembly. Stops for the lower drawers can be made form scrap plywood and should be attached to the desk base with glue and brads. Three 13-5/16-inch long scrap pieces will be needed so as to fit in place between the two dividers at a point 16" in from the front of the desk.

A "pigeon hole" type assembly is used to form the upper drawers, resulting in a 5-drawer unit. The entire assembly is made from 1/2" birch plywood, including the six 3"x6-1/4" dividers which are set at equal distances apart. Assembly calls for glue and 3d finishing nails. Set the nail heads and cover with matching wood filler. Cover all exposed plywood edges with flexible wood trim.

The "pigeon hole" upper drawers assembly is attached to the desk top, which is cut to a 23-1/2"x42" size from 3/4" fir plywood. Glue and No. 8x1" flathead wood screws are used to attach the assembly to the desk top. The top is then attached to the lower drawer dividers with glue and 4d finishing nails. Set the nail heads and cover with wood filler.

Having cut the desk side pieces to plan size and contour from 1/2" birch plywood, the next step is to attach plywood spacers to each side piece to form ends for the lower drawer compartments. The spacers are cut from 1/4" fir plywood and are 3-3/4"x16" in size. Glue and brads are used to attach the spacers to the side pieces.

The contoured 42" desk back is attached to the side pieces, the desk top, desk base, and upper drawer unit with glue and 3d finishing nails. Cover the nail heads with wood filler and cover all exposed plywood edges with flexible wood trim.

The upper and lower drawers are typical box-type assemblies. Fir plywood is used, the upper drawer fronts being made of 1/2" stock, while the lower drawer fronts are of 3/4" stock. Sides and backs are 3/8" plywood. Drawer bottoms are made from 1/8" hardboard. Glue and 3d finishing nails are used to assemble the drawers. All dimensions are shown on the plan.

Sand and finish the desk as desired.

(Note: To obtain the full-size pattern for this project, order Trestle Desk Pattern #435.

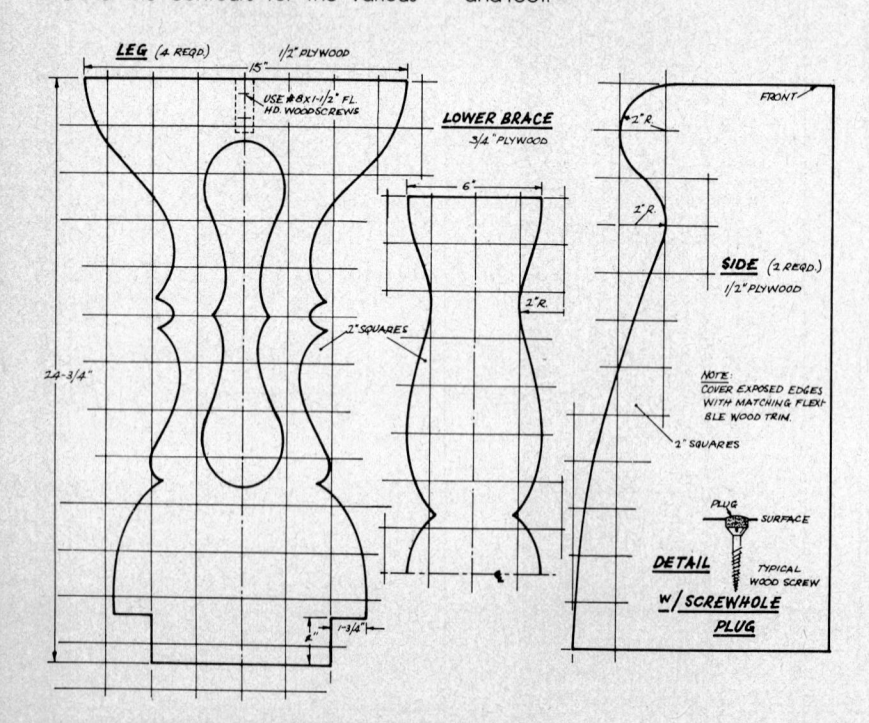

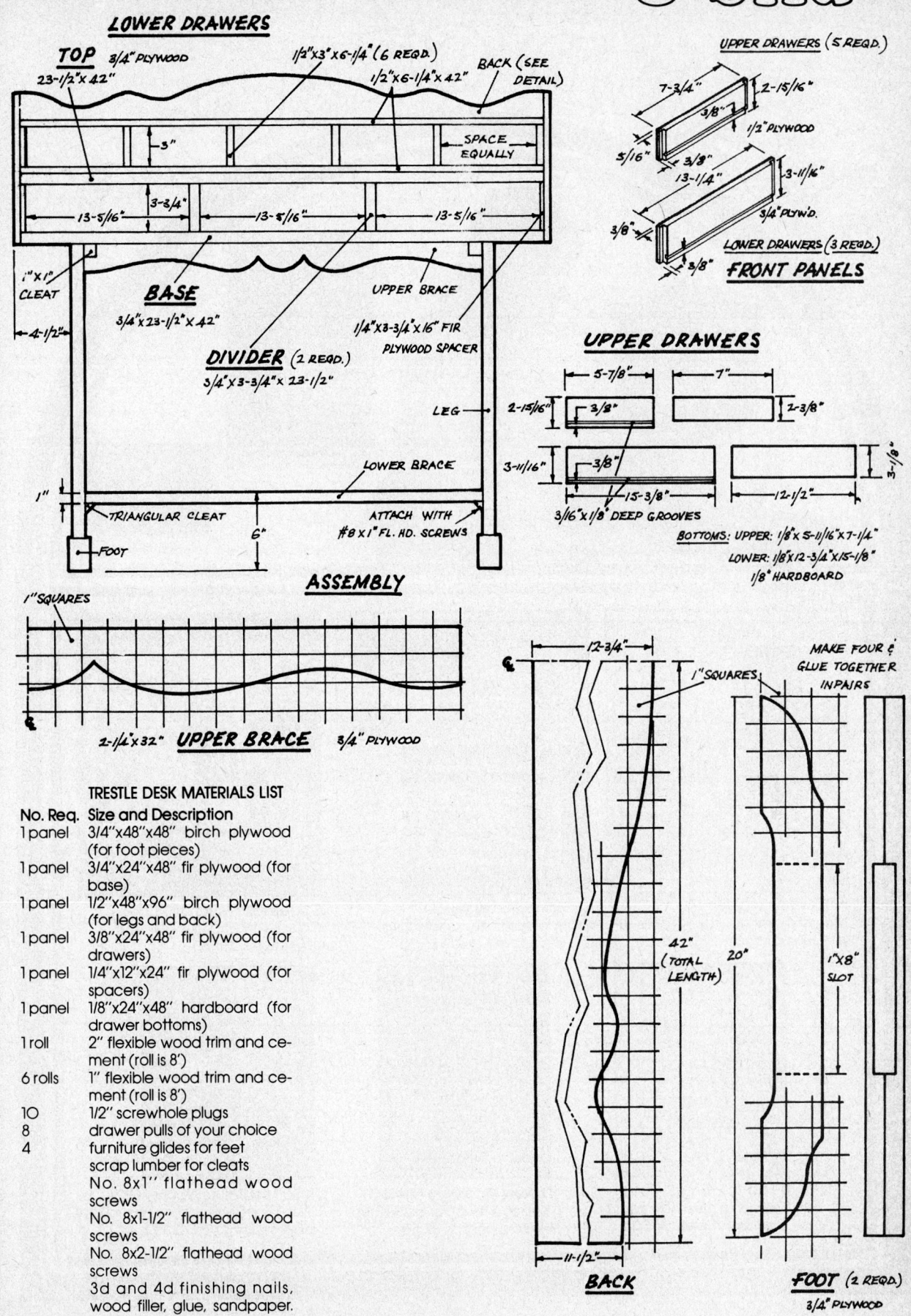

U-bild

LOWER DRAWERS

TOP 3/4" PLYWOOD
23-1/2" x 42"
1/2"x3"x6-1/4" (6 REQD.)
1/2"x6-1/4"x42"
BACK (SEE DETAIL)
SPACE EQUALLY
3"
3-3/4"
13-5/16"
1"x1" CLEAT
4-1/2"
BASE 3/4"x 23-1/2"x 42"
DIVIDER (2 REQD.) 3/4"x 3-3/4"x 23-1/2"
UPPER BRACE
1/4"x 3-3/4"x 16" FIR PLYWOOD SPACER
LEG
LOWER BRACE
1"
TRIANGULAR CLEAT
FOOT
6"
ATTACH WITH #8 x 1" FL. HD. SCREWS

ASSEMBLY

UPPER DRAWERS (5 REQD.)
7-3/4"
2-15/16"
3/8"
1/2" PLYWOOD
5/16"
13-1/4"
3-11/16"
3/4" PLYW'D.
3/8"
3/8"

LOWER DRAWERS (3 REQD.)
FRONT PANELS

UPPER DRAWERS
5-7/8"
7"
2-15/16"
3/8"
2-3/8"
3-11/16"
3/8"
15-3/8"
12-1/2"
3-1/8"
3/16"x 1/8" DEEP GROOVES

BOTTOMS: UPPER: 1/8"x 5-11/16"x 7-1/4"
LOWER: 1/8"x 12-3/4"x 15-1/8"
1/8" HARDBOARD

1" SQUARES
2-1/4"x 32" **UPPER BRACE** 3/4" PLYWOOD

TRESTLE DESK MATERIALS LIST

No. Req.	Size and Description
1 panel	3/4"x48"x48" birch plywood (for foot pieces)
1 panel	3/4"x24"x48" fir plywood (for base)
1 panel	1/2"x48"x96" birch plywood (for legs and back)
1 panel	3/8"x24"x48" fir plywood (for drawers)
1 panel	1/4"x12"x24" fir plywood (for spacers)
1 panel	1/8"x24"x48" hardboard (for drawer bottoms)
1 roll	2" flexible wood trim and cement (roll is 8')
6 rolls	1" flexible wood trim and cement (roll is 8')
10	1/2" screwhole plugs
8	drawer pulls of your choice
4	furniture glides for feet
	scrap lumber for cleats
	No. 8x1" flathead wood screws
	No. 8x1-1/2" flathead wood screws
	No. 8x2-1/2" flathead wood screws
	3d and 4d finishing nails, wood filler, glue, sandpaper.

12-3/4"
1" SQUARES
MAKE FOUR & GLUE TOGETHER IN PAIRS
42" (TOTAL LENGTH)
20"
1"x 8" SLOT
11-1/2"
BACK
FOOT (2 REQD.)
3/4" PLYWOOD

43

HANDICRAFTS

A. Tole Painting (#U104)
Use acrylic paints, tracing carbon and full-size patterns. $2.50

C. Stained Glass (#H601)
From lampshades to windows. 50-page color guide. $5.00

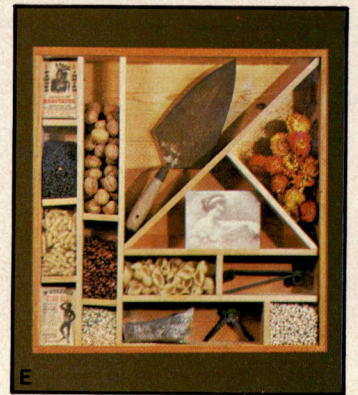

E. Keepsake Hutch (#532)
Complete instructions. Fill with collectibles. $1.00

B. Fabric Frames (#U110)
24 color pages show you 13 different styles. $3.50

D. New Macrame (#H450)
32-page full-color book. Step-by-step photos. $2.50

F. Soft Sculpture Dolls (#SP22)
Step-by-step directions and full-size patterns for 11 dolls. $3.75

A. Wooden Ornaments and Creche (#U111)
Capture the spirit of Christmas past by creating wooden ornaments and this nativity scene from wooden beads and dowels. This 24-page guidebook includes step-by-step directions and photos for 19 tree decorations including a train, angel, clown, teddy bear, rocking horse, and more. **$3.50**

B. Traditional Quilting (#SP25)
Full-size patterns for 12 historical quilting designs are included in this 15-page guidebook. Instructions for making a lap frame also included. **$3.75**

C. The Rag Doll Book (#HA42)
Create 10 different rag dolls which stand approx. 11" tall. Patterns for their clothes as well! **$3.00**

D. How to Sew a Quiet Book (#SP11)
Keep young ones occupied while they learn basic coordination and to differentiate between shapes, colors and numbers. You create the quiet book by following this 15-page instructional guide. **$3.75**

Other Sewing Guides you may enjoy:
#SP12 Sew a Country Kitchen $3.75
#SP23 Kitchen Witch Faire $3.75
#SP24 Machine Embroidery $3.75
#SP38 Darlin' Dolls $3.75
#SP42 Countryside Geese $3.75
#SP43 Soft Character Clowns $3.75
#G457 Sock Bunnies $5.00
#G463 Fabric Ducks $5.00
#G464 Quilt Hoops $5.00
#G468 Pocket Teddy Bears $5.00
#G470 Tiny Tots $5.00
#G474 Collectable Dolls $6.00
#G483 Doll Clothes $5.00
#L102 Fabric Wallets $4.00
#L107 Horses & Unicorns $4.00

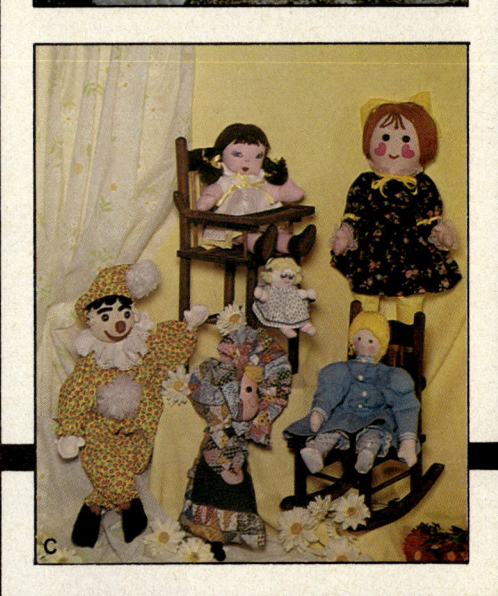

A. Pinecones: Gifts of Nature (#U103)
Create a naturally-beautiful holiday atmosphere in your home. **$2.50**

B. Christmas Crafts & Wraps (#U106)
Step-by-step directions for a jeweled tree, bows and ornaments. **$2.50**

Other Holiday Craft Books:
#H454 Old Fashioned Christmas $4.00

C. Drying Flowers With Household Products (#U105)
Dry flowers with laundry detergent, etc. then display them. **$2.50**

Also Available:
#GM27 Flower Arranging $3.00
#GM39 Brides Silk Flowers $3.00

D. Jeweled Ming Trees (#H238)
Create jeweled trees with beads, shells and gold wire. **$3.75**

E. Egg Carton Flowers (#H190)
23-page guidebook leads you step-by-step in creating from plastic egg cartons. **$3.75**

F. How to Make Plant Hangers (#H420)
This 33-page guidebook shows you how to create a variety of hangers by simply tying different knots. **$2.50**

Other macrame patterns available:
#547 Macrame **$2.00**
#GM16 Christmas Macrame **$2.50**
#G423 Elegant Macrame **$2.50**
#HH33 Classic Macrame **$3.75**

G. Choose 'N Fuse (#M641)
Create such charming creatures as this cougar, a sly fox, lion, parrot and more. Fusing is a new handicraft technique using braided polycord. **$2.50**

H. Decorating With Collectibles (#H229)
Turn old and discarded objects into decorator items with the help of paint, decals and ribbons. **$3.75**

I. Spinning Wheel (#662)
Spinning your own yarn is a relaxing and fruitful hobby. The wheel measures 30"lx34"h. Full-size traceable pattern makes it easy. Also available, Spinning Wheel Kit . . . pre-cut and ready to assemble, **$150.00** (incl. shipping). Write for more information.

J. 3-D String Art (#552)
Full-size pattern has a variety of abstract designs. Simply wrap threads around nails. **$2.00**

K. Americana Weaving (#HA57)
Weave wall-hangings, pillows, tablemats, etc. Step-by-step instructions for on-loom and off-loom techniques. **$2.00**

47

LATEST PROJECTS

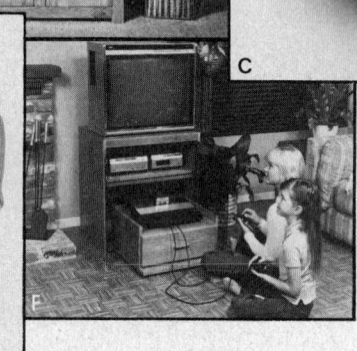

A. Linen Closet (#735)
3 large shelves on top, 2 smaller ones on bottom. 68" tall, 28½" wide, 13¼" deep.

B. 3-Drawer Oak File Cabinet (#727)
44" high x 19" wide x 21" deep. Step-by-step instructions.

C. Butler's Table (#717)
All four leaves lock upright. Open, table measures 30" wide x 42" long x 17" high.

D. Kitchen Utility Center (#749)
Stands approx. 6' high and is on casters. Will easily hold your microwave oven.

E. Blanket Chest (#724)
A seating bench and storage for blankets, linens, etc. 20" h x 20" w x 47" l.

F. VCR/Video Game Cabinet (#754)
Will house your T.V., VCR, video game player, joysticks, tapes, and game cartridges in one unit 26¾" w x 21¾" d x 28¼" h.

KEEP THIS STUB AS A RECEIPT
(see other side)

FOR MORE INFORMATION REGARDING PATTERNS, PLANS, GUIDEBOOKS, ORDERING, OUR CURRENT CATALOG, CUSTOMER SERVICE, ETC., PLEASE WRITE TO:

U-BILD • P. O. BOX 2383 • VAN NUYS, CALIFORNIA 91409

TEAR OR CUT ALONG THIS LINE

READ ALL ABOUT IT!
Over 700 Easy-to-Do Projects

are pictured in the 112-page catalog, PATTERNS FOR BETTER LIVING. Now, with the help of Steve Ellingson's simple step-by-step patterns and plans, you can create anything from a macrame wallhanging to a mountain cabin. Lawn furniture, interior furnishings, children's toys, recreational equipment, even handicrafts. You name it, there's a U-BILD PLAN that helps you build it yourself.

Only **$2.95** (includes postage)

HOT OFF THE PRESSES!

You'll enjoy our popular 160-page CHILDREN'S TOYS & FURNITURE book, #FM7, containing step-by-step plans for 50 different projects . . . **$7.95** (incl. postage).

TO OBTAIN EITHER BOOK, SEE REVERSE SIDE

FOLD HERE

Name _____
Street _____
City _____
State _____ Zip _____

PLACE STAMP HERE

U-BILD
P.O. Box 2383
Van Nuys, CA 91409-2383

RECEIPT OF ORDER

Pattern or Book Numbers Ordered:

_____ _____ _____ _____ _____ _____ _____

_____ _____ _____ _____ _____ _____ _____

Date Ordered: _____

Total of Order: $ _____

Check or Money Order: # _____

TEAR OR CUT ALONG THIS LINE

9305 _____

Name _____

Street _____

City _____

State _____ Zip _____

1st CLASS POSTAGE & HANDLING

Total Amount of Order	1st Class
Up to $3.00	1.00
3.01 to 5.00	1.50
5.01 to 7.50	2.00
7.51 to 10.00	2.50
Over $10.00	Add 25%

California residents please add 6% sales tax.
Canadian orders must be accompanied by U.S. funds.

PATTERN OR BOOK NO.	QTY.	DESCRIPTION	PRICE EACH	TOTAL

Total of Goods Ordered $ _____

Less 10% for orders of $10.00 or more $ _____

Subtotal $ _____

California residents add 6% sales tax $ _____

Shipping & Handling Charges (see chart above) $ _____

GRAND TOTAL $ _____

Oak Furniture Classics (#C55)

This classic collection includes three popular antique oak reproductions. The lawyer's bookcase is stackable... you choose whether it's 2, 3, or 4 shelves high. An oak file cabinet which will even hold legal-size hanging files. And the third member is the old favorite oak ice box. Retail Value — $9.00
Special — $5.75

Please print name and address and enclose check or money order for your pattern selection.

☐ Check here for $2.95 U-Bild Catalog (price includes bulk postage)

☐ Check here for $7.95 Children's Toys & Furniture Book

All Pattern Prices are $3.00 Unless Marked Otherwise
(plus postage)

THIS FLAP IS GUMMED — SIMPLY FOLD, SEAL & MAIL

A. Doll Carriage (#719)
Sturdy, yet lightweight, it holds a standard-size baby doll. 27½" l x 9½" w x 26½" h. Full-size traceable pattern.

B. Rocking Elephant (#750)
"Peanuts" measures 31" l x 17" w x 20" h. Safety features include limited rocking motion, foot pegs, rounded edges.

C. Wooden Toy Trucks (#737)
A steamshovel, tractor and flatbed truck with trailer. Steamshovel bucket and tractor blade move up and down.

D. Child's Rocker (#734)
Begin a new family tradition with this oak rocker. 25" high, with a 15" wide seat. Step-by-step traceable pattern. **$3.50**

E. Kiddy Copter (#720)
Step-by-step directions show you how to cut all parts from ¼" and ⅝" plywood.

F. Pony Rocker (#738)
Smooth, rounded edges and a yarn tail and mane make this safe for all children. A real favorite!

$3.00 ... ALL PATTERN PRICES ARE $3.00 UNLESS OTHERWISE MARKED
(Plus postage – see chart on page 112)

A. & B. Travel Table & Stools (#751)
Venture into lovely remote areas to enjoy your outings and be self-sufficient with your own table and stools. Folded, the table measures 47½ x 41 x 5½ . . . open it seats 4-6 and measures 47½ x 28 ½ 29. Set-up takes only minutes. **$2.50**

C. Arbor Settee (#753)
Plan includes traceable patterns for the arch, lattice-work, and side panels. Stands 97½" high, 98" wide and 40" deep . . . seats two adults. **$3.50**

D. Single-Door Ice Box (#723)
Authentic-looking icebox reproductions are being used more and more by home decorators. A bar, home filing cabinet, or end table. 26"h x 23"w x 17"d. **$2.00**

E. PVC Twin-Seater (#726)
Smart, durable, and easy to clean. Approx. 63" long, 23" deep and 23" tall. Uses standard-size cushions. Step-by-step directions and photos.

F. Birdhouse Trio (#731)
A martin castle, chickadee hut and wren chalet. They can easily be placed on a pole platform, or be hung in a tree. Easy-to-do with our step-by-step directions & photos. **$3.50**

G. Large Windmill (#739)
It stands a gracious 9' high with a base that extends to 5 feet. Rear door allows access to limited storage space and the turret revolves on a large bearing. **$3.50**

H. Apothecary-Style Chest (#714)
This storage cabinet measures 33" high, 30" wide and 15" deep. Its 16 small drawers can store an array of items in the home workshop, sewing room or den.

50

A. Stereo Components Center (#725)
Featuring tinted glass doors, this oak cabinet will house your tuner/amplifier, tape deck and tapes. Shelves are adjustable. 45" high x 24" wide x 20" deep.

B. Game/Lamp Table (#728)
The table measures 24" square and stands 26" tall. The reversible game board has chess on one side and backgammon on the other. Directions for a cribbage board also included.

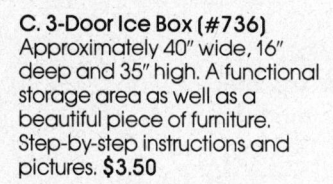

C. 3-Door Ice Box (#736)
Approximately 40" wide, 16" deep and 35" high. A functional storage area as well as a beautiful piece of furniture. Step-by-step instructions and pictures. $3.50

D. Multi-Purpose Home Desk (#744)
Perfect for a home-computer or typewriter this desk measures 53" wide x 22" deep x 27½" high. Included in the plan is a matching elevator stand to hold your video screen at eye level. $3.75

E. Captain's Bed (#747)
Made from pine and mahogany plywood, holds a 39" x 75" twin mattress. Two drawers 6" x 22" x 22" offer ample space for storing clothes. Traceable pattern included for headboard. $3.50

F. Moveable Closet Organizer (#743)
Build this project and move it into your closet to achieve maximum use of closet space. When you move, it goes with you!

G. Armoire (#729)
Another piece in our lovely bedroom suite, it measures approximately 39" wide, 21" deep, and 77" tall. Plenty of hanging space on top and a large pull-out drawer on the bottom. $3.50

H. Rollaround Multi-Purpose Table (#746)
The perfect companion for any home or office. Can hold the printer for your home computer or simply provide extra work space.

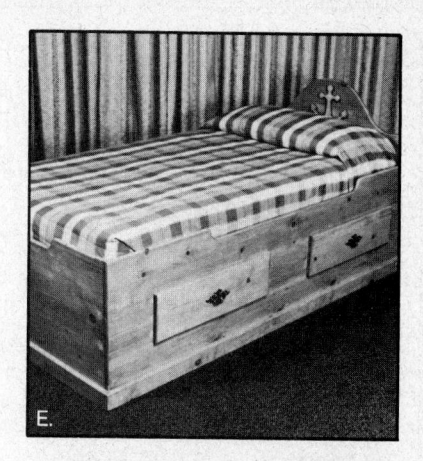

51

U-bild mini-plan

The sturdy little rocker pictured here (Photo 1) is a perfect gift for children on their birthday, or any occasion for that matter. The miniature chair is something a young son or daughter can call their very own. Not only will the rocker be a joy to present as a gift, it will be easy for the father or grandfather who has a shop at home to build.

The entire rocker is constructed from 3/4" birch plywood or any other veneer plywood desired. One piece, measuring 48" square, is all that is needed.

Use the squares method to transfer the shape of the side of the rocker to the plywood (Fig. 1). The sides can be cut out on a band saw or scroll saw. Note that both sides are cut at one time by tacking the two pieces of plywood together (Photo 2).

A table saw or radial saw is used to cut the rocker back, the seat board (Fig. 2), and the arm rests (Fig. 3) to shape. A 4° angle is required on the sides of the seat board (Photo 3), as well as on the ends of the front (Fig. 4) and rear braces. These are also cut on a table or radial saw. A taper cutting jig is needed to cut the sides of the back panel (Photo 4). Note the 4° angle on the bottom edge of the back (Fig. 5). The design on the back is cut out with a scroll saw or band saw. Cut the arm rest notches on the table saw or radial saw. If a table saw is used, set the miter gauge at 11-1/2° to the right for the right arm rest and 11-1/2° to the left for the left arm rest. Use a stop clamp to ensure uniformity in the cuts on both arm rests (Photo 5). If a radial saw is used, the arm is rotated 11-1/2° to the right and left to make the angle cuts.

Photo 1: A rocking chair for youngsters.

MATERIALS

Quantity	Description
2	3/4" x 20" x 25-1/2" Sides
1	3/4" x 12-1/2" x 16" Back
1	3/4" x 12-7/8" x 13" Seat board
2	3/4" x 2" x 12" Arm rests
1	3/4" x 3/4" x 13" Rear brace
1	3/4" x 1-1/2" x 13-1/2" Front brace
16	No. 6 x 1-1/2" Flathead wood screws
2	No. 6 x 1-1/4" Flathead wood screws
4	5d Nails
18	Screw hole plugs
10	Hardwood dowels

Child's Rocker Mini-Plan courtesy of Robert Scharff & Associates, Ltd.

Photo 2: Cutting out both sides of the rocker on a band saw in one operation, after transferring the shape to the plywood, using the squares method.

NO. 6 X 1 1/2" FL. HD. WOOD SCREWS

CHAIR BACK

NO. 6 X 1 1/4" FL. HD. WOOD SCREWS (FASTEN ON INSIDE)

ARM REST

NO. 6 X 1 1/2" FL. HD. WOOD SCREWS

25 1/2"

NOTE: ALL SCREWS ARE RECESSED WITH PLUGS

WOOD SURFACE
PLUG

ASSEMBLE SEAT BOARD TO BACK USING 5d FINISHING NAILS

ASSEMBLE SIDES & BRACES TO SEAT USING NO. 6 X 1 1/2" FL. HD. WD. SCREWS

SEAT BOARD

REAR BRACE

13"

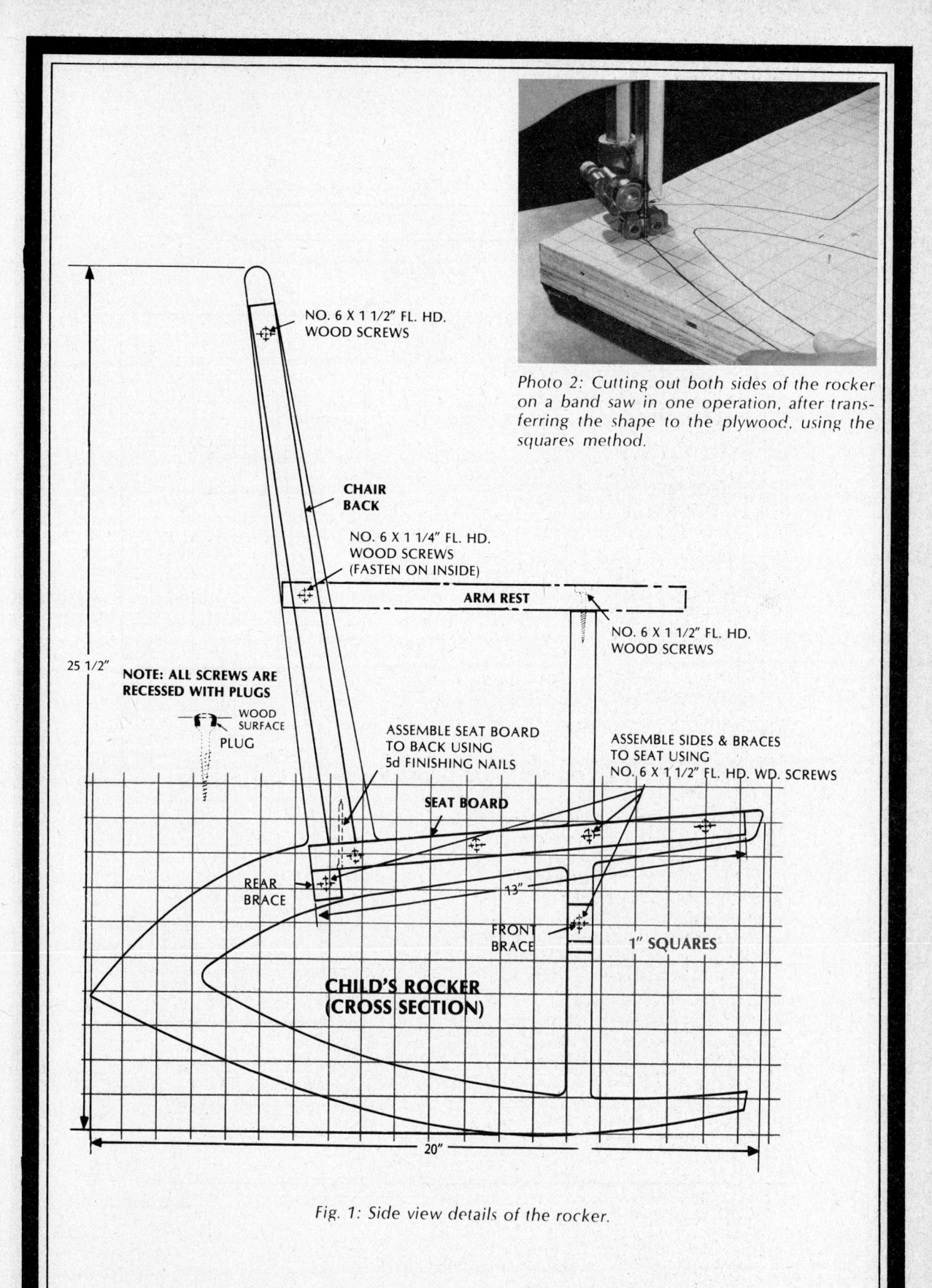

FRONT BRACE

1" SQUARES

CHILD'S ROCKER (CROSS SECTION)

20"

Fig. 1: Side view details of the rocker.

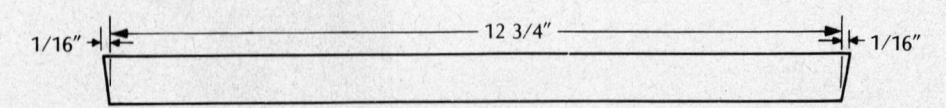

Fig. 2: Seat board details.

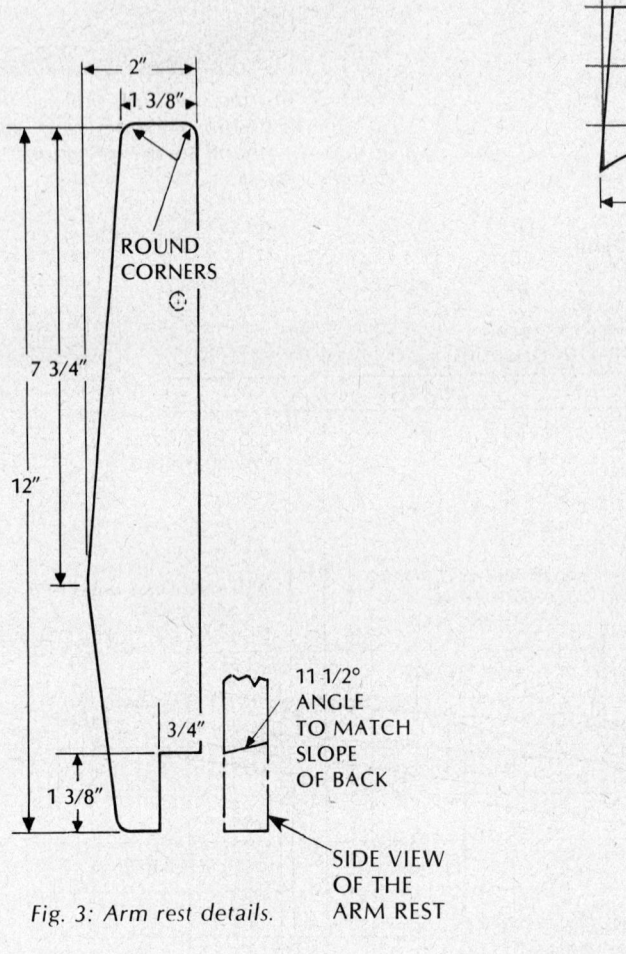

Fig. 3: Arm rest details.

ROUND CORNERS

11 1/2° ANGLE TO MATCH SLOPE OF BACK

SIDE VIEW OF THE ARM REST

1" SQUARES

Fig. 5: Details for the back of the rocker.

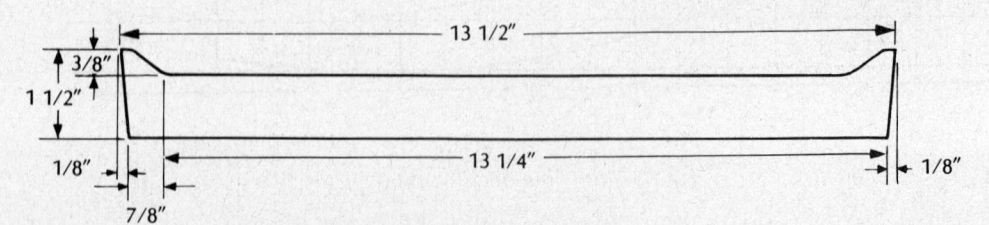

Fig. 4: Front brace details.

Photo 3: Cutting a 4° angle on the sides of the seat board. Note: Blade guard removed for clarity.

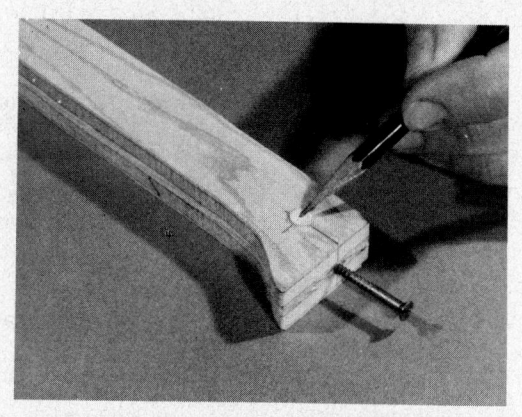

Photo 6: Screwing into a hardwood dowel gives added strength when screw fastening into end grain.

Photo 4: Using a taper cutting jig on a table saw to cut the sides of the back. Note: Blade guard removed for clarity.

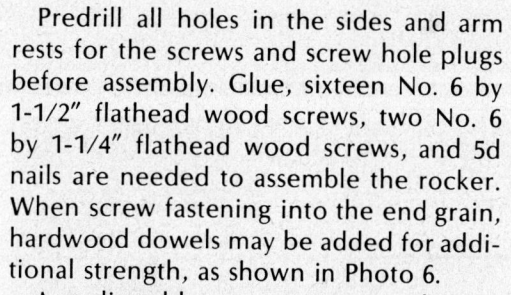

Photo 5: Cutting the notches in the arm rests on a table saw; a stop clamp ensures the uniformity of the cuts. Note: Blade guard removed for clarity.

Predrill all holes in the sides and arm rests for the screws and screw hole plugs before assembly. Glue, sixteen No. 6 by 1-1/2" flathead wood screws, two No. 6 by 1-1/4" flathead wood screws, and 5d nails are needed to assemble the rocker. When screw fastening into the end grain, hardwood dowels may be added for additional strength, as shown in Photo 6.

An adjustable screw setter greatly simplifies the assembly of the rocker. In one operation, it predrills, countersinks, and counterbores for the flathead wood screws and wood plugs used in the assembly.

Flexible wood veneer makes it easy to cover the exposed plywood edges. The veneer, also called edging tape, is fastened with contact cement. Apply it with hand pressure, then tap it down with a rubber headed mallet to achieve a good bond. Make sure all of the corners are rounded and any sharp edges are sanded smooth. Complete the project with a clear semi-gloss wood finish, sanding lightly between coats.

A 12" by 12" knife edge or box style cushion will add comfort and enhance the beauty of the project.

To obtain full-size traceable pattern, order pattern #392 . . . $3.00

KIDS 'N' PETS

A. Antique Fire Truck (Pattern #634)
Clever updating of old-fashioned fire truck. Measures 40"l x 22"h. Uses foot power.

B. Dump Truck (#682)
This realistic toy truck moves by pedal power and has a working dump lever. Great fun for kids!

C. Kryon Star Flyer (#696)
This spaceship pattern features pedal power and lettering for the instrument panel. $3.50

D. Kiddy Tractor (#610)
Foot power and axle-rope steering insure safety. 36" long by 18" high, with full-size pattern.

A. Jeep (#410)
Simple in design and of sturdy construction. Just trace the full-size pattern and cut out.

B. Big Rig (#715)
A pedal-powered vehicle for little truckers. Accessories available in auto/bike stores.

C. Bulldozer (#716)
Foot-powered and moves on 4" wheels and casters. Plan includes traceable parts.

D. Panel Truck (#383)
Step-by-step directions and photos make this one a cinch. Becomes a mail, milk or any delivery truck.

E. Airplane Swing (#491)
Hang from a tree or build the support frame detailed in the pattern.

$3.00 ... ALL PATTERN PRICES ARE $3.00 UNLESS OTHERWISE MARKED
(Plus postage – see chart on page 112)

mini-plan

A little bundle of joy squalls its way onto the American scene approximately every 10 seconds. No question about it, there's lots of activity in the nursery these days.

Along with the activity has come many innovations in nursery furnishings. No longer need the baby's room be an island of uninteresting, obviously practical baby equipment. New nursery furnishings are now designed not only to aid busy mothers, but to harmonize with other furnishings in the home.

The baby's cradle, for instance, need not be a stark hospital-like combination of austere bars and boards. No reason at all when you can build one yourself that is just as good looking as your other furniture pieces. The cradle shown here has charm, but what is more, it's relaxing for baby as a rocking chair is for adults.

The cradle shown was made of birch plywood, but you may select any one of dozens of darker fancy plywoods, depending upon your other furnishings. This one is equipped with casters which make it easy to move from one room to another. The size is standard to fit a regular baby mattress.

(To order full-size pattern, see coupon on back page. Specify No. 300

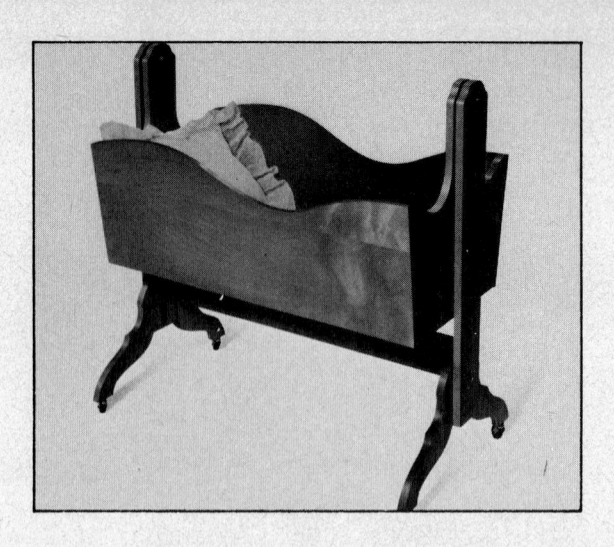

CRADLE MATERIALS LIST

No. Req.	Size and Description
1 panel	3/4"x4'x4' hardwood veneer plywood (birch, mahogany, etc.)
1 panel	1/2"x3'x3' hardwood veneer plywood
1 pc.	1/4"x1'x2' hardwood plywood
4	No. 10/2" flathead wood screws
6	No. 10/1-1/4" flathead screws
2	1/4-20, 2" machine bolts with washers and nuts
2	1/4x20 Teenuts
	2d, 3d finishing nails, glue, finishing stain or enamel
4	casters (if desired)

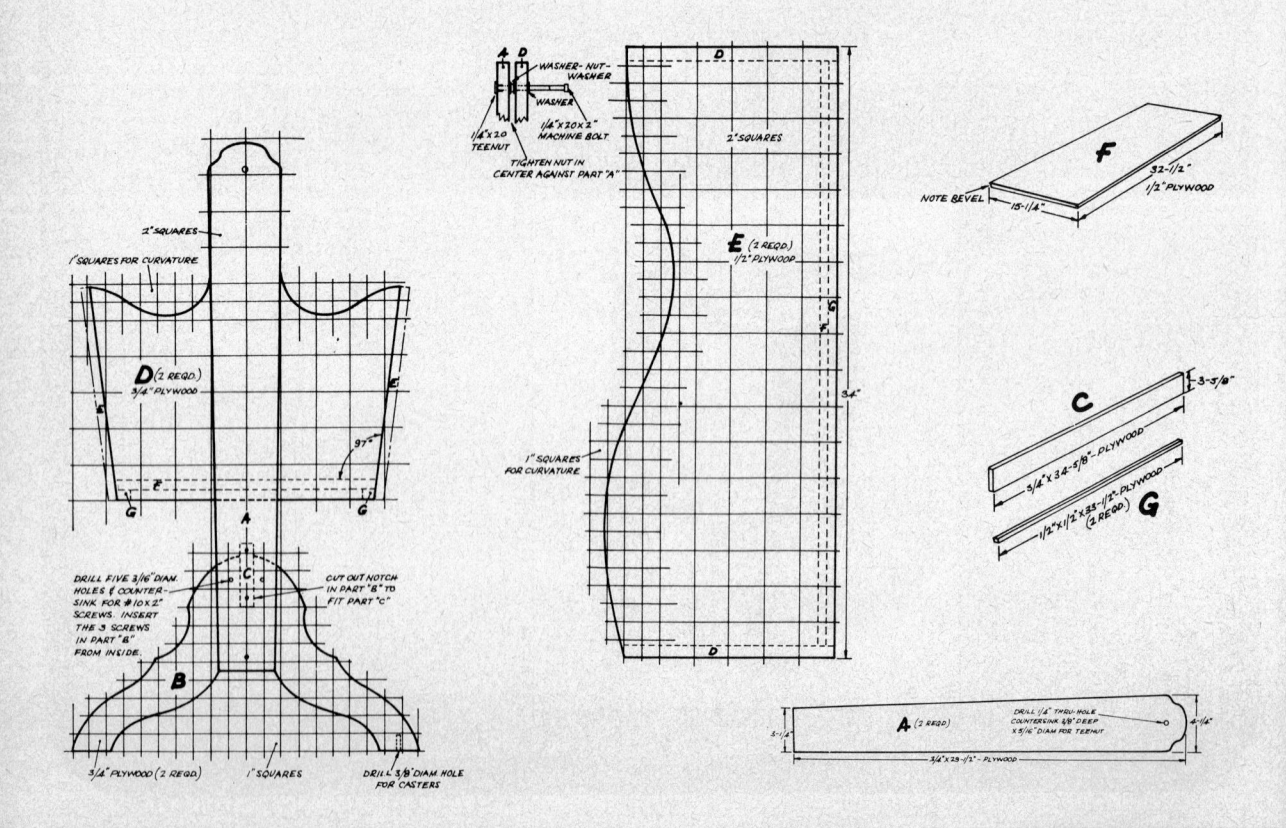

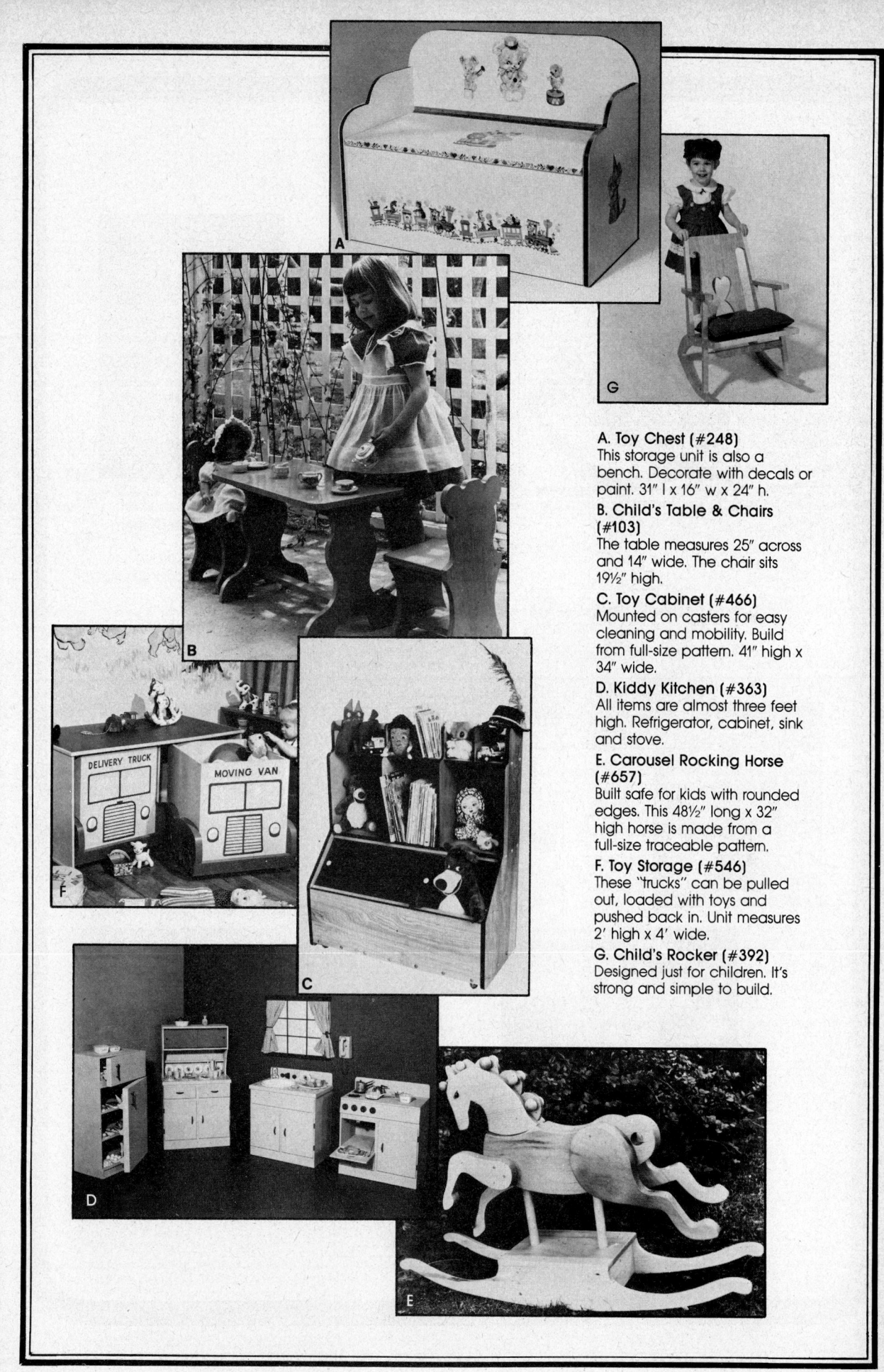

A. Toy Chest (#248)
This storage unit is also a bench. Decorate with decals or paint. 31" l x 16" w x 24" h.

B. Child's Table & Chairs (#103)
The table measures 25" across and 14" wide. The chair sits 19½" high.

C. Toy Cabinet (#466)
Mounted on casters for easy cleaning and mobility. Build from full-size pattern. 41" high x 34" wide.

D. Kiddy Kitchen (#363)
All items are almost three feet high. Refrigerator, cabinet, sink and stove.

E. Carousel Rocking Horse (#657)
Built safe for kids with rounded edges. This 48½" long x 32" high horse is made from a full-size traceable pattern.

F. Toy Storage (#546)
These "trucks" can be pulled out, loaded with toys and pushed back in. Unit measures 2' high x 4' wide.

G. Child's Rocker (#392)
Designed just for children. It's strong and simple to build.

A. Rocking Horse (Pattern #56)
Full-size pattern shows how to build either rocking horse or elephant. 29"x24."

B. Pony Rocker (#131)
Designed for small children. Strong and safe. **$2.00**

C. Clothes Rack (#113)
Stands about 44" tall with rounded pegs on neck to hang clothes. **$2.00**

D. Circus Wagon (#718)
18" wide x 38" long x 33" high, this toy box will hold any child's stuffed critters and toys.

E. Cat Castle (#388)
Designed for cat's natural love of high places. Step-by-step directions. **$2.00**

F. Doghouse/Playhouse (#733)
Saloon or barn-style on one step-by-step plan. **$3.50**

G. Dog House (#299)
Accommodates any size dog. Top lifts off and doors swing out. **$2.00**

H. Barn Dog House (#448)
Mounted on casters for mobility. Small roof can be removed to clean.

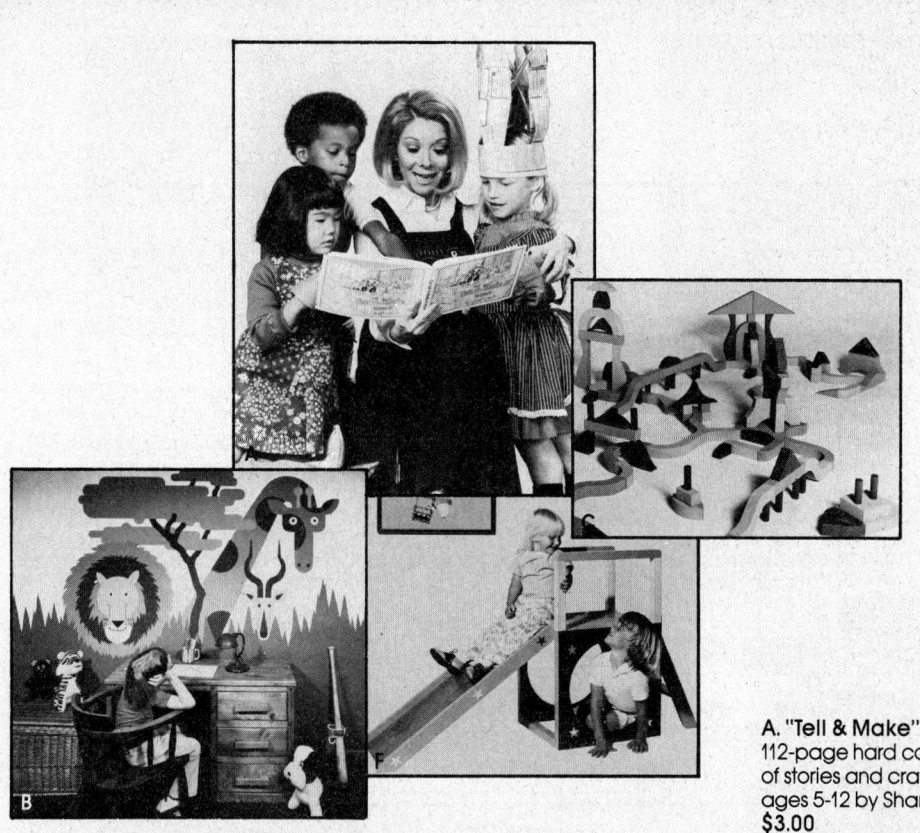

A. "Tell & Make" (#584)
112-page hard cover book of stories and crafts for kids ages 5-12 by Shari Lewis. **$3.00**

B. Jungle Wall Mural (#588)
Iron this full-size pattern onto your wall and paint. **$4.00**

C. Building Blocks (#384)
Blocks are cut from 2 x 12 lumber. Pattern for cart included.

D. Wooden Toys (#632)
A paddle-driven steamboat, an antique car, and an airplane.

E. Jungle Pin-Ups (#679)
Make plaques or trace onto wall and paint. Full-size patterns for all 5 included.

F. Indoor Slide (#580)
This safe, sturdy slide measures 20" wide, 36" high and 61" long. Easy-to-build.

$3.00 ... ALL PATTERN PRICES ARE $3.00 UNLESS OTHERWISE MARKED
(Plus postage – see chart on page 112)

A. Doll House (Pattern #310)
All four roof panels swing up for easy acccess to interior. 57" x 40" and set on casters.

B. Dollhouse (#607) & Doll Furniture (#606)
Made using full-size patterns. Scale 1"=1'

C. The Harrison Doll House Kit
Pre-cut wood construction. Up to 9 rooms. 37"w x 21"d x 31"h. **$89.95** (including shipping).

D. Revolving Doll House (#329)
Turns so that any room can be brought around to play in. Made from ¼" plywood.

E. Open Back Doll House (#411)
Stands 24½" tall and 20" across. Full-size pattern makes this one a cinch.

F. 11½" Doll House (#697) & Matching Furniture (#698)
Made just for fashion-model dolls. Provides hours of fun.

G. 11½" Doll Furniture (#361)
Includes patio, living room, bedroom plus tote-about wardrobe.

H. Victorian Doll House (#671)
House front opens to show six rooms with fireplace and stairway. Step-by-step directions.

A. Little Red Barn (#461)
Measures 6' x 8' and is simple to build. Perfect outdoor playhouse.

B. Alpine Playhouse (#658)
Irrestible with its "gingerbread" style. It stands 7' tall with a 4' x 4' playing area.

C. Red Schoolhouse (#619)
44-1/2" square and almost 4' tall. Traceable pattern even includes belfry and bell.

63

RECREATION

A. Deluxe Bar (#481)
Also a breakfast bar and ice-cream fountain. Can be built any length. Easy-to-follow pattern includes photos and clear directions.

B. 3-in-1 Vacation Pak (#518)
Camper, boat and cartop carrier provides 36 cubic feet of handy travel space. The capsule rides easily on top of car.

C. Deluxe Pool Table (#475)
Easy-to-build and smartly styled, this pool table is a welcome addition to any home. Detailed plan for 86"x48" table.

D. Cedar Sauna (#563)
Measures approx. 4'x6' and houses a self-contained heater within insulated walls. No special wiring needed.

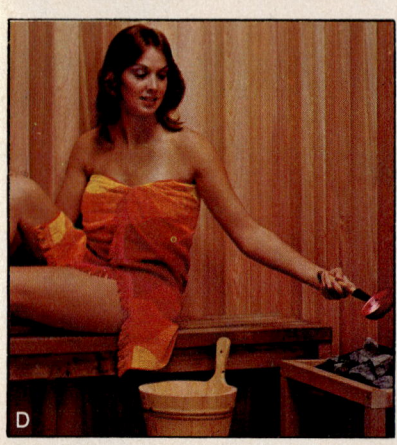

A. Deck Boat (Plan #578)
This easy-to-build twin hull deck boat is 22' long and has over ten feet of open deck space and 40 cubic feet of storage. Uses marine plywood.

B. Miniature Sailer (#398)
Two panels of fir plywood and one weekend are all you need to build this sturdy 5-foot sailer. Step-by-step directions guide you.

C-D. Catamaran (#559)
This 14' cat is built from 1/4" plywood and requires no special tools. Easily disassembled (without tools) for transporting. Uses a 98 sq. ft. sail.

E. Huck Finn Raft (#534)
Weighs 50 lbs. and can be carried on a cartop. Holds 4 pint-sized sailors and uses an inner tube plus foam flotation system.

F. Pram Dinghy (#399)
Strong, all-purpose dinghy weighs only 79 lbs. and measures 7'9" long. Fits on a cartop and is easy for children to row.

G. Knockabout (#380)
A safe, stable sailboat for family fun. This 15-footer is made from exterior fir plywood by following a simple plan.

$3.00 ... ALL PATTERN PRICES ARE $3.00 UNLESS OTHERWISE MARKED
(Plus postage — see chart on page 112)

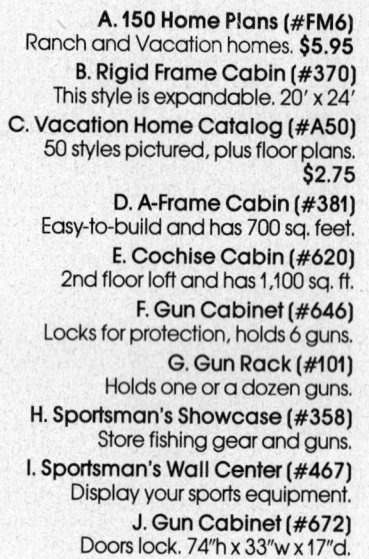

A. 150 Home Plans (#FM6)
Ranch and Vacation homes. $5.95
B. Rigid Frame Cabin (#370)
This style is expandable. 20' x 24'
C. Vacation Home Catalog (#A50)
50 styles pictured, plus floor plans.
$2.75
D. A-Frame Cabin (#381)
Easy-to-build and has 700 sq. feet.
E. Cochise Cabin (#620)
2nd floor loft and has 1,100 sq. ft.
F. Gun Cabinet (#646)
Locks for protection, holds 6 guns.
G. Gun Rack (#101)
Holds one or a dozen guns.
H. Sportsman's Showcase (#358)
Store fishing gear and guns.
I. Sportsman's Wall Center (#467)
Display your sports equipment.
J. Gun Cabinet (#672)
Doors lock. 74"h x 33"w x 17"d.

F

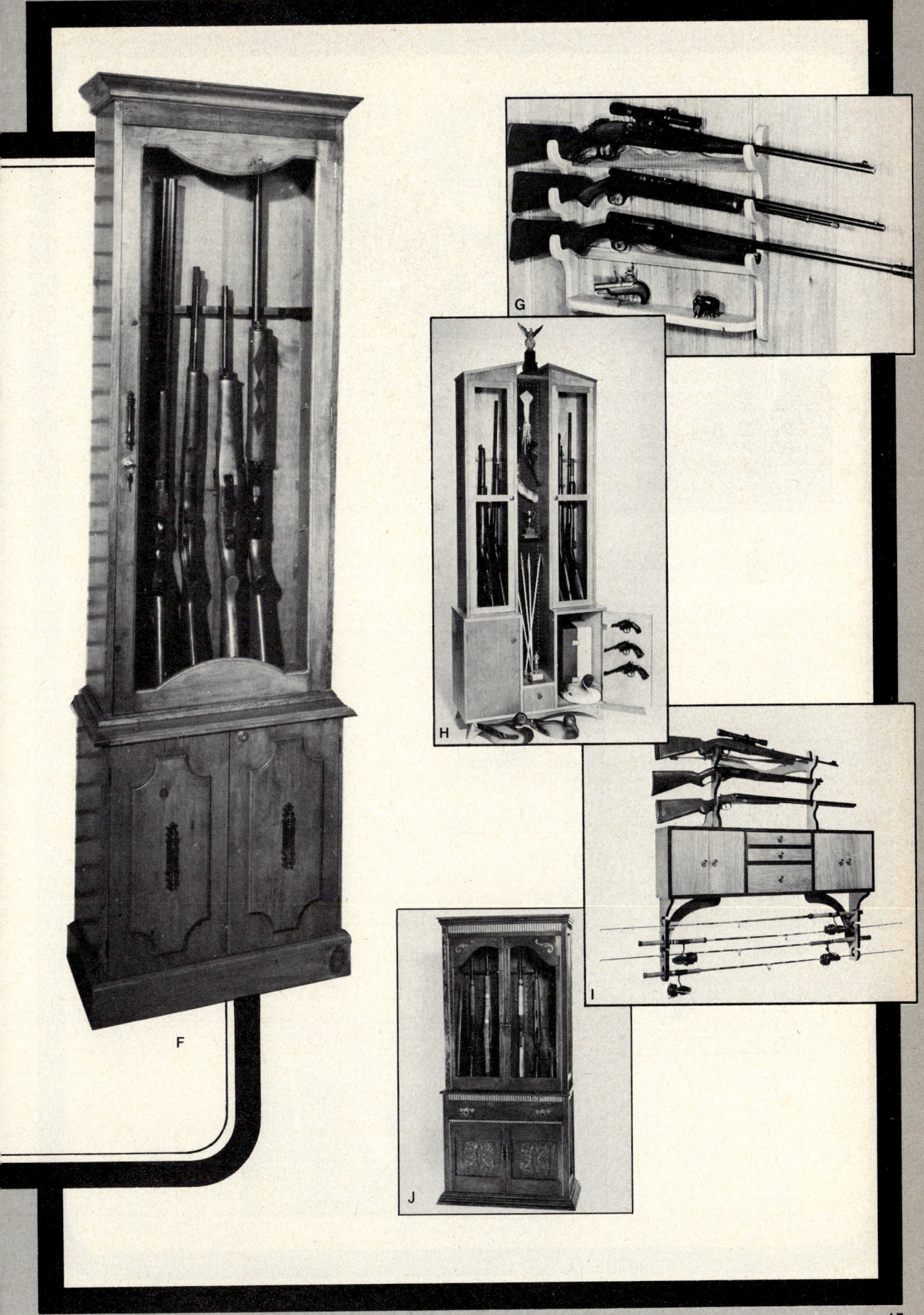

G

H

I

J

67

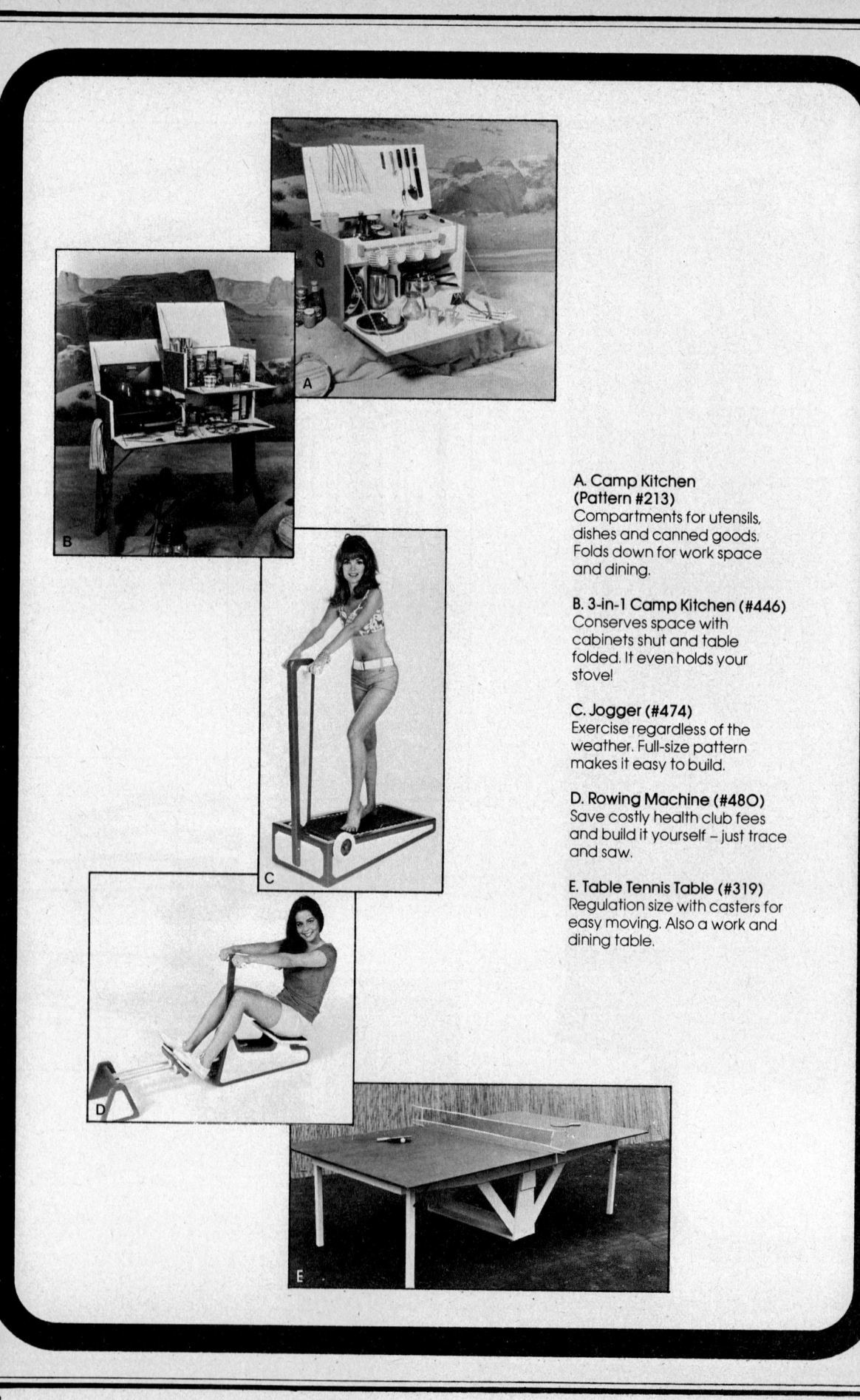

A. Camp Kitchen (Pattern #213)
Compartments for utensils, dishes and canned goods. Folds down for work space and dining.

B. 3-in-1 Camp Kitchen (#446)
Conserves space with cabinets shut and table folded. It even holds your stove!

C. Jogger (#474)
Exercise regardless of the weather. Full-size pattern makes it easy to build.

D. Rowing Machine (#480)
Save costly health club fees and build it yourself – just trace and saw.

E. Table Tennis Table (#319)
Regulation size with casters for easy moving. Also a work and dining table.

U-bild mini-plan

Whatever your plans for this year's vacation—whether you're looking forward to the mountains or the woods, the lake or the sea shore—you can expect more fun and less worry if you have a safe place for your baggage.

The problem for most travelers isn't getting there and back—it's finding a place to pack everything. We have noticed cars on the road that are so full of luggage that there isn't room for people. That's hardly the way to get away from it all.

Some tourists pile their luggage in a rack on top of their car; a good idea too, until it rains. If you cover the luggage with a canvas, more often than not, it becomes loose and begins to flap in the wind. That's not the way to have peace of mind on a trip. Furthermore, it isn't good looking.

The thing we need is a rain, snow, dust and wind proof luggage compartment that can be locked and carried on top of the car. We can relax and enjoy the ride when we know our possessions are protected both from the weather and thieves. The compartment shown here was designed with these factors in mind. Besides that, it's good looking and may be painted the same color as your car. You will notice it has a hinged top which makes it easy to pack and unpack. The size may be varied depending upon your specific needs.

(To order full-size pattern, see coupon on back page. Specify No. 228).

LUGGAGE CARRIER MATERIALS LIST

No. Req.	Size and Description
1 panel	1/4" x 4' x 8' Fir plywood, exterior type, for parts G, H and I
21 ft.	1 x 12 pine for parts A, B, C, D, E & F
6 ft.	1 x 2 Pine for Parts J
3 ft.	Piano hinge and screws
28 in.	Light chain with screws (for stop)
2 pcs.	Suitcase catches and screws
	4d finishing nails, 3d galvanized nails and 3/4" wire brads
	Waterproof glue, sandpaper, plastic wood and finishing materials

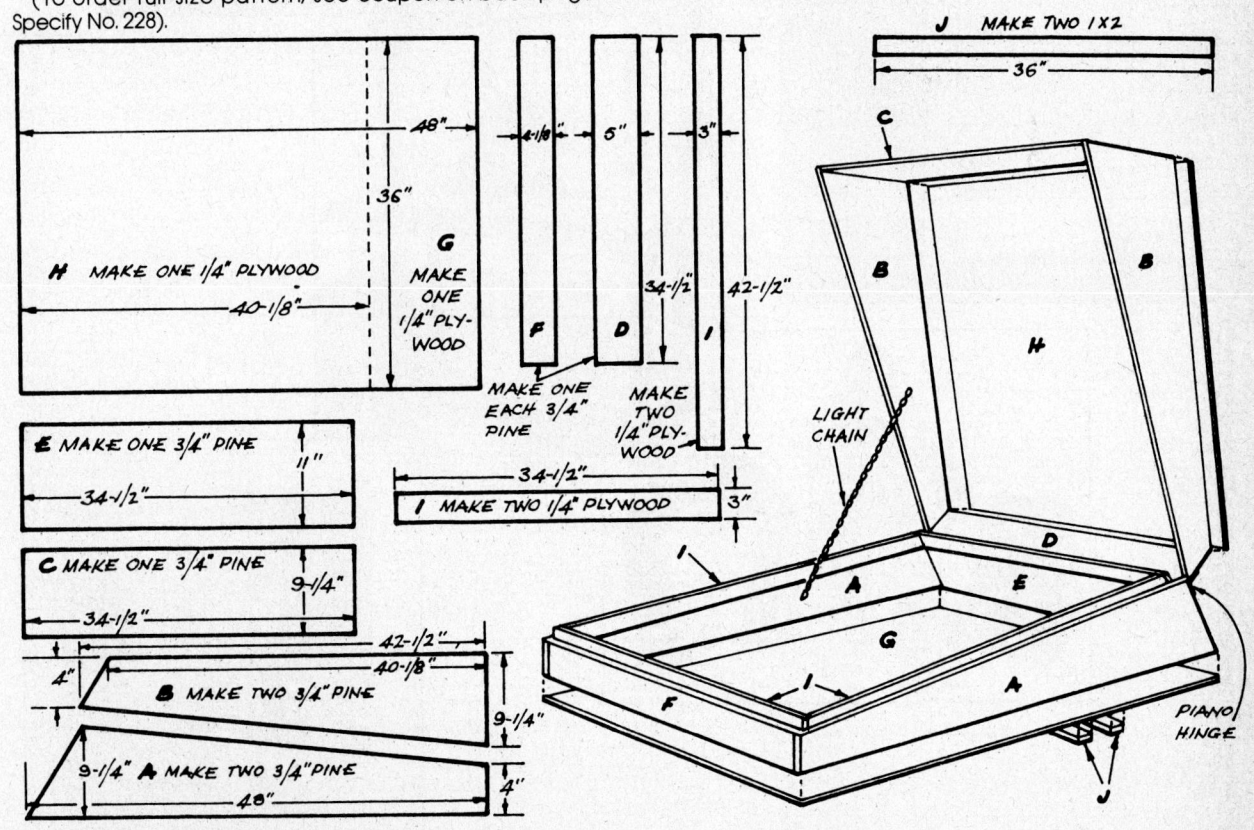

A. Ice Box (Plan #686)
This authentic reproduction holds glassware in the top and stores bottles down below.

B. Rustic Bar (#519)
Or Mediterranean style! Optional overhang approx. 7' high. Photos guide you.
Bar stool (#284).

C. Wine Rack Trio (#528)
Full-size patterns for all 3 styles. Built mainly of plywood.

D. Wine Cellar/Liquor Cabinet (#260)
Removable diagonal shelves, built on casters and hinged in the middle.

E. Wet Bar (#651)
Measures 60" l x 18" w x 40" h but modular in style. Instructions include finishing front.

F. Table Soccer (Plan #654)
Playing field is 2' wide and 3' long. Includes instructions on players, parts & game.

G. Pool Table (#417)
Measuring 8' x 4' x 36" high, this model has a ball return system.

H. Poker Table (#217)
Has pockets for chips and drinking glasses . . . or seats 8 for dinner.

I. Mini-Pool Table (#473)
Only half the size of regular pool tables. Easy-to-build. 48" x 32" x 36" high.

J. Wine Cabinet/Serving Table (#645)
Approx. 5' long, this handsome piece stores your favorite wines. Removable racks.

$3.00 . . . ALL PATTERN PRICES ARE $3.00 UNLESS OTHERWISE MARKED
(Plus postage — see chart on page 112)

U-bild

Your Home Workshop

The Basic Dozen

Compiling a list of basic tools is like creating a meat loaf recipe, people know what you are talking about but everyone has a different idea of what the ingredients should be. However, the 12 tools suggested cover measuring, cutting, holding and fastening functions common to all repair jobs.

For accurate measurements, select a retractable steel tape at least 10 feet long. It's handy, flexible and can be locked in position. The 12-inch combination square with a small level in the sliding head has both 90 and 45-degree angles. Rip saws cut along the wood grain; cross-cut saws at right angles. Since most projects require lumber trimmed to length, or you work with "grainless" plywood or hardboard, a rip saw is often unnecessary. Select a 26-inch long, 10-point crosscut. A utility knife with replaceable blade in the handle will cut linoleum, carpeting, roofing and cardboard. The half-round wood rasp can shape and smooth wood prior to final sanding.

For driving and pulling nails, a 16-ounce curved claw hammer and a nail set are essential. Metal, fiber glass or wood handles are available. A dropforged, bell faced head is recommended. Drill starting holes and drive screws with one tool. The combination screwdriver and push drill has interchangeable square and Phillips head screw blades and several size drills stored in the handle.

A sturdy pair of wire cutting pliers and an 8-inch crescent wrench are handy for electrical, auto and bike repairs. A 2-inch bladed putty knife is ideal for those patching, puttying and scraping chores. For the dollar invested, a 1/4 or 3/8-inch portable electric drill is one of the best tool buys. Get one with variable speed and reverse capabilities. Buy a set of small twist bits and then add larger spade bits as needed.

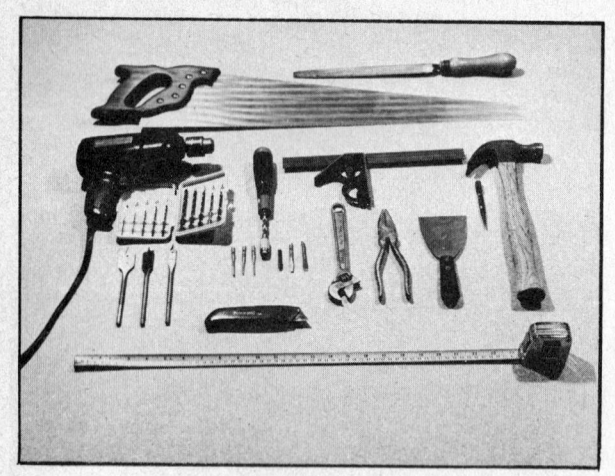

A basic set of 12 hand tools makes up a survival kit which enables a homeowner with average skills to handle simple maintenance and repair projects.

Intermediate Tool Selection

Here are a few extra tools which will increase your ability to handle larger and more complex projects. For remodeling or room additions, a rafter or framing square and an aluminum level, 24 inches long with horizontal and vertical bubbles, are invaluable. The large square with 16 and 24-inch legs is used for establishingangles and laying out stud, rafter and joist spacing. On remodeling jobs in older homes where walls and floors have usually settled out of square, it is frequently more important to determine plumb (vertical) or level (horizontal) lines than a square angle.

Clamps provide an extra hand when measuring or gluing material. Spring and small bar clamps are inexpensive, quick and come in several sizes. A single clamp is usually inadequate for many jobs so buy a pair in several sizes. For minor plumbing problems, arc joint pliers are adjustable for standard fixture sizes and have a jaw capacity up to 4 inches. A 14-inch pipe wrench with milled teeth is designed to lock onto pipes up to 2 inches in diameter. Long or needle nosed pliers with side cutters are great for snipping wire, forming electrical connections and handling a variety of delicate holding tasks. Straight bladed tin snips cut sheet metal, window screening, wire fencing, leather, rubber and plastic materials. Buy a quality drop forged steel set with hardened cutting edges for long life.

High carbon steel wood chisels are used for everything from general shop work to hanging a door. Buy them separately or in sets with 1/4, 1/2, 3/4 and 1-inch wide blades. Nothing beats a sharp bench plane for smoothing a board edge or trimming a sticking door to the right size. An all purpose 9-inch long bench plane with a 2-inch wide blade is a good choice. The final suggestion for your expanded tool collection is a small hand sanding block with flat bottom surface, rounded and angled edges.

Hand Power Tools

Compact, inexpensive power tools are the answer to the homeowner who wants to complete repair and creative projects in a professional and quick manner. After the portable electric drill, a portable circular saw is often the next choice. A 7-1/2-inch blade model will fashion straight, bevel and miter cuts in stock up to 2 inches thick with ease. A smaller cousin, the sabre saw, also cuts bevels and miters but has the added capability of cutting curves, circles and fancy designs.

Smooth, well-sanded surfaces are necessary if you hope to achieve a good final finish. Lower priced hand sanders have an orbital or slightly circular action. For a few dollars more, you can buy a dual-action sander with orbital action for rough sanding and, by flipping a lever, straight line action for that

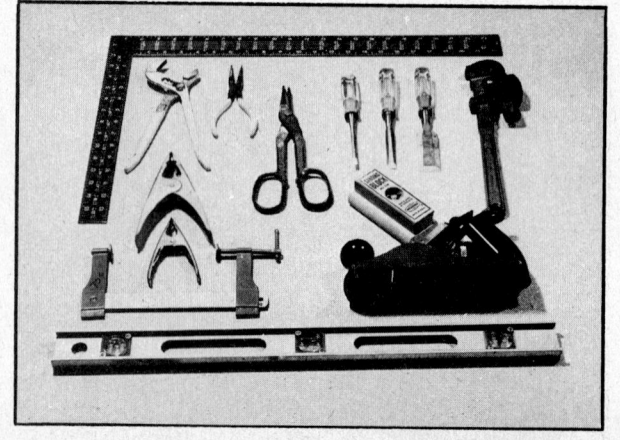

As your skills develop and projects expand, an additional set of tools will permit you to tackle more difficult jobs successfully.

U-bild

final with-the-grain finish sanding. For those tough jobs where a lot of material must be removed, a powerful belt sander does the job in a hurry.

One of the most creative power tools is the router. Dozens of different router bits allow you to shape wood surfaces and edges in a variety of designs. Create your own signs, trim plastic laminates or mold a professional edge on your cabinet doors with a router.

Today's low cost, high quality hand power tools are a good investment. They not only save time on larger jobs but provide a professional touch to your work.

As your tool collection expands, you may want to add several hammers and mallets, a miter box and saw, chalk and plumb line, bevel and contour gauges, stapler, wrecking bar, small block plane and long pipe clamps.

Workshop Locations

Garages and basements are the two most popular locations. The basement is usually warm, convenient and wired for power and light. But it can be damp, cramped for space and difficult to control noise, sander dust and finishing odors. The garage with a large door provides easy access and your construction activities normally won't intrude on family living. However, you'll probably have to add power and lighting, be concerned with security and you may find yourself constantly fighting with the family car for working space. If you live in a rural area, an existing barn or outbuilding can be converted into a fine workshop. If you have room in a suburban lot, consider building a separate shop structure. Or in a mild climate, use a paved carport area with a utility shed for storage. Within the home itself, a little used porch can be enclosed and a spare bedroom or attic space turned into a shop. Folding or wall hinged workbenches can often be installed in a family or utility room but this is only a temporary work space. Carefully planned compact workshops have been built in storage areas under stairs and into closets.

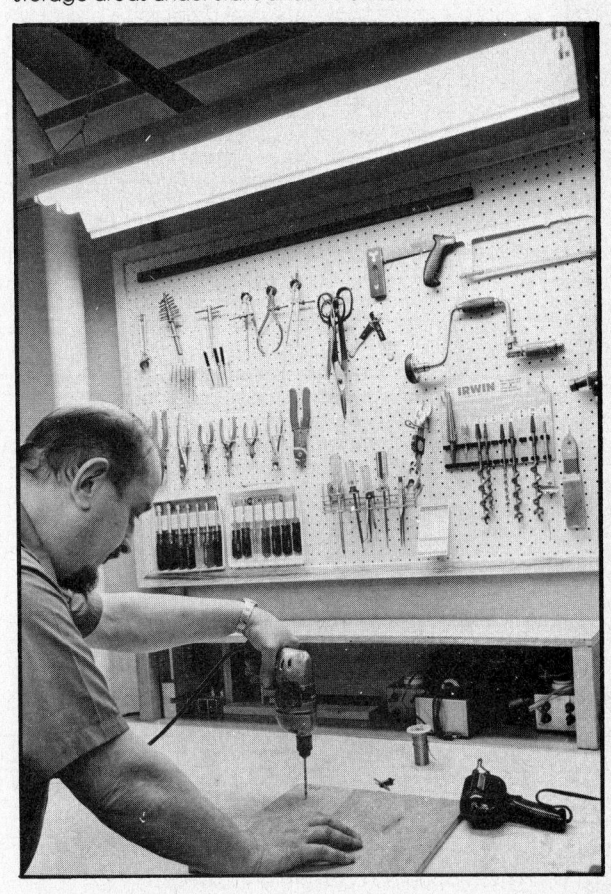

Two 40-watt fluorescent tubes directly over the work surface supply even, glare free lighting. Fixtures use little power and are easily installed. Photo-General Electric

Overcoming Shop Problems

Flooded or damp workshops present serious problems. Not only will tools quickly rust, but everytime you reach for the light switch or plug in a power tool, you risk an electrical shock. Sump pumps can control minor flooding and epoxy waterproofing applied to walls and floors will check dampness. Serious cases may require dehumidifiers or space heaters to discourage rust. Acoustical tile and fiber glass insulation in ceilings and walls will reduce the noise level within the shop. Controlling vibration also helps reduce noise. Workbenches should be firmly attached to the wall or floor, power tools should have sturdy, level bases. Rubber pads or carpeting mounted between the base and motor will help overcome excessive noise. A tight, well-fitted shop door, preferably solid core rather than hollow, will reduce both noise and dust problems. Dust collectors on saws and power sanders speed shop cleanup time and a roll around vacuum is a good housekeeping investment. For both safety and security, the shop door should have a lock or if this is not possible, put a lock on several drawers and cupboards. Lay out your shop carefully to allow adequate work space, efficient tool placement and provide lots of room to manuver around large projects. Shop doors should be at least 36 inches wide. Direct access from outdoors to your shop is ideal but not always possible. If you find yourself staggering through the back door, down the stairs, around the corner and through the game room before you get that plywood panel into your shop, well, you have a problem. Installing a new basement entrance is somewhat expensive but often worthwhile.

U-bild

Workshop Wiring

Since you will probably add power tools in the future, equip your shop now with more power than you need. And remember to keep your lights and power on separate circuits. It's bad enough when your saw runs into a knot, jams and blows a fuse, but on a single circuit setup, you're also left standing there in the dark. Power strips with multiple outlets can be mounted on the workbench, along the wall or even overhead. Duplex outlets can be placed conveniently in several locations throughout the shop. All outlets should be grounded and capable of accepting three-prong plugs. A master switch that shuts off all shop cicuits is a sound safety precaution.

Adequate shop lighting improves accuracy, provides an important safety factor and makes the shop a more pleasant place to work. The level of illumination is measured in "footcandles" and the average shop requires a minimum of 80-100 footcandles for efficiency and comfort. If you are establishing your shop, incandescent bulbs with reflectors are less expensive. But in the long run, fluorescent tubes will give you 2 to 4 times as much light for the same amount of energy. Some stationary power tools like grinders, band saws and drills have built-in lighting, but use a handy clip-on portable light to wipe out shadows for close work. Although most local building codes permit a homeowner to do wiring, if you have any doubt about the proper method, it's smarter to use the services of a professional electrician.

Workshop Safety

Shop safety is basically a matter of common sense. Work intelligently and eliminate hazards before they become serious accidents. Clothing should be comfortable, but remove dangling neckties, roll loose sleeves and if you wear a shop apron, be sure tie strings are in the back. Eliminate anything that interferes with your work or that could be caught up in a revolving power tool. Good lighting and a clean floor and bench top will help avoid accidents. Safety goggles or a full face mask will protect eyes when grinding or sawing. Inhaling spray paint fumes or sander dust can be harmful to nose and lungs, so wear a filter mask for safety. Lock your shop if possible or at least keep sharp edged and power tools beyond small fingers. Power tools can present special hazards, so become familiar with each tool and don't push it beyond its rated capacity. Some tools feature removable key plugs, or you can prevent unauthorized use by installing a small padlock through the plug prongs.

A large two-sided bench in a basement workshop is divided by vertical tool storage panels. Good lighting, acoustical walls and ceiling and built-in drawers make this an attractive and efficient workshop for the serious homeowner.
Photo-Masonite Corp.

Duplex outlet box is wired beneath bench top. A small shelf stores hand power tools close to the power source and to the bench top work surface.

Your workbench is the heart of the shop and therefore the first and most important piece of furniture. Bench plans are available from lumber and plywood associations, various tool manufacturers and your Public Library has books and magazines featuring workbench construction plans. When you find a plan, chances are you will make some modifications to meet your specific needs, so keep the following points in mind. For an average 5-foot-10-inch-tall individual, the bench top should be approximately hip-joint high or 36 inches from the floor. Tops are from 24 to 30 inches wide and as long as space permits. For solid, wobble-free construction, use screws or bolts plus glue rather than nails. Leave an inch or two overhang around the top edge for clamping purposes. A good utility vise with 3 or 4-inch jaws should be bolted to the left or righthand front edge of the bench. Over the years, the top will receive tough wear, so a replaceable hardboard or linoleum surface is often used. Better yet, face the top with maple or oak flooring. A strip of electrical outlets can be placed along the back wall, but it's more convenient to attach to the front or side edge of the bench. This keeps the top free of cords while you're working. Bolt the bench to the floor or wall for stability. Since you saw down on a board, the sawhorse is lower than the bench, about 24 inches off the floor. Either buy metal brackets or use 2 x 4-inch lumber to make your own pair of horses. Floor stands for larger power tools are built with 2 x 2 or 2 x 4-inch lumber legs. Again, use screws or bolts plus glue for rigidity. Slant legs about 7-degrees from the vertical for added stability. In small shops, put casters on legs, so equipment can be rolled aside when not in use.

U-bild
THE RIGHT TOOLS FOR THE JOB

Shop built band saw base on casters has 2x3 legs and plywood sides. Table saw base, with 2x2 legs, uses cut-out top so sawdust drops into box below. Both bases have legs angled 7-degrees from vertical to add stability. Plywood tool box is a time and step saver for around the house repair jobs.

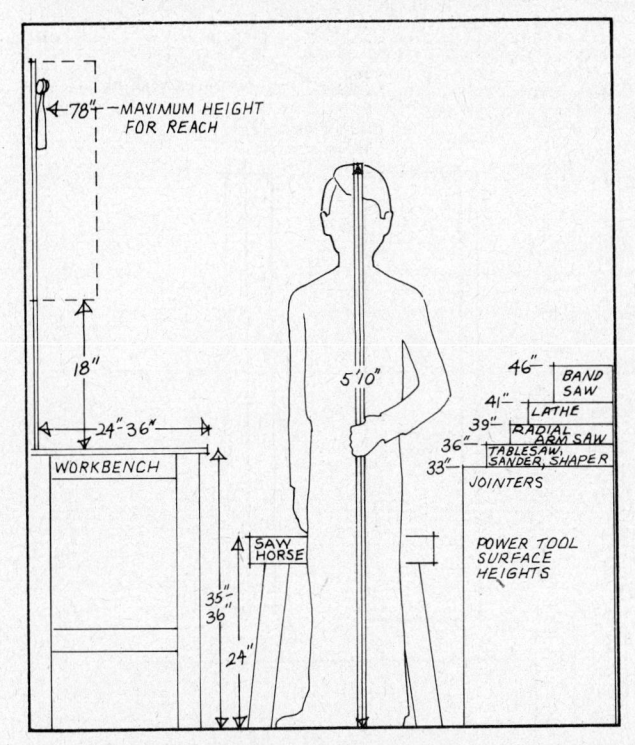

For maximum efficiency and comfort, the American National Safety Institute recommends the following average table heights for various shop equipment: jointers – 33 inches; table saws, shapers and sanders – 36 inches (since table saws and jointers are often used together, place them side-by-side on the same base); radial-arm saws – 39 inches; lathes – 41 inches and band saws – 46 inches.

Job to be done	Appropriate hand tools	Useful power tools
Cutting round hole	hand drill, brace, keyhole saw, file, compass	jig saw, drill and hole-saw, fly cutter
Cutting square opening	ruler, keyhole saw, hand drill	jig saw, drill
Fastening to masonry	star drill, hammer, dowel, masonry bolts	1/2" drill, carbide-tipped drills
Fastening to hollow wall	Molly bolts, drill, screwdriver	drill
Fastening to wood	drill, awl, hammer, screwdriver	drill
Securing loose brick	cold chisel, hammer, mortar, whiskbroom	
Repairing rotted clapboard	saw, chisel, hammer, nail set, pry bar, paint and brush	circular or jig saw
Repairing popped nails in drywall	pliers, nails, hammer, nail set, plaster mix	
Patching hole in plaster wall	saw, knife, plaster mix, metal lath, sandpaper, primer	
Stopping pipe leak	pipe clamp, wrench, screwdriver	
Loosening binding door	screwdriver, dowels, shims, plane	
Replacing broken window pane	chisel, hammer, glazier's point, paint, sandpaper, glass	
Replacing sash cord (with chain)	screwdriver, chisel, hammer, chain, knife, string and weight	
Loosening stuck window	hammer, putty knife, wax	
Replacing socket or switch (after turning off current)	screwdriver, socket or switch, tape	
Replacing defective lamp plug	new plug, cutting pliers, knife, solder, soldering gun, flux, tape	
Replacing frayed lamp wire	new wire, screwdriver, cutting pliers, knife	
Correcting wobbly table or chair	lengthen leg with wood shim, glue and brad or cut down with fine saw	
Tightening loose chair rung	glue, long clamp	
Removing cigaret burn on rug	wire brush	vacuum cleaner
Unclogging stopped drain	toilet plunger, lye solution, wrench, pail	
Securing loose or missing ceramic wall tile or fixture	awl, plaster mix, tile, rag	
Pasting down loose wallpaper	wallpaper paste, scissors, water, rag	
Anchoring loose floor tile	putty knife, chisel, hammer, sandpaper, tile cement	
Removing floorboards	nail set, saw, hammer, chisel, pry bar	circular saw
Curing a squeaky floor	drill, screw-type nails, counter sink, hammer	drill
Sanding floor	scraper, sandpaper, nail set, hammer, pry bar	belt and disk sander, vacuum cleaner
Installing door	chisel, gauge, hammer, drill, awl, plane, screwdriver	drill, router
Installing door lock	brace, drill, chisel, hammer, screwdriver, awl	drill, router, hole saw
Fixing loose handle	dowel, glue, drill, awl, screwdriver	drill

U-bild mini-plan

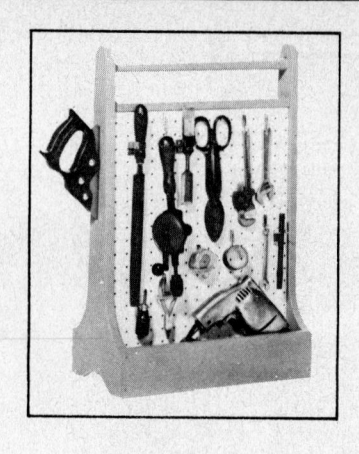

This project will help in several ways. First, it provides a neat compact workshop for the home handyman. Second, it's an incentive for the man of the house to do his own odd jobs rather than hiring someone to do them.

We call this a tool caddy. The caddy has two different sides which will hold as many as 35 different tools. The tools are fastened on pegboard with clips which are available at all hardware stores. You will notice that the tools are all in plain sight and easy to get at.

The saw is inserted between the sides where the teeth are protected. At the bottom, a space is provided for glass jars which will contain screws, nails, bolts, nuts and things of that kind.

You will find that it's much easier to take your tools to the job than it is to take the job to your tools. The caddy requires but little storage space. It's good looking and we'll guarantee it's as handy as anything ever invented for the home handyman (or handy woman).

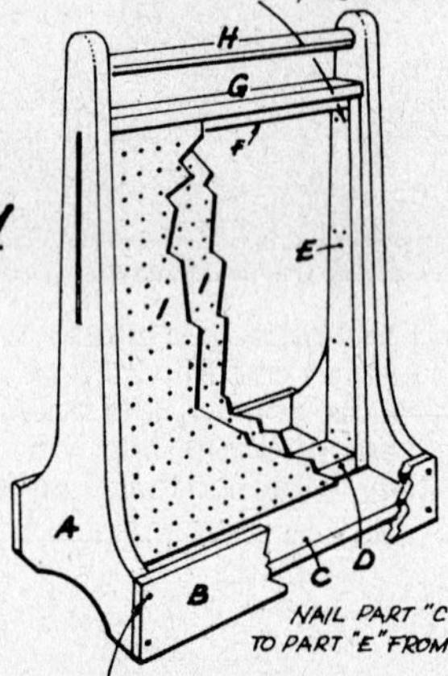

TOOL CADDY MATERIALS LIST

No. Req.	Size and Description
1 pc.	1" x 10" pine board, 6' long, select grade, knot-free or with very small tight knots (for Parts A, B, C, D, E, F, and G)
1 pc.	1/2" x 4" pine board, same as above, for part B
1 pc.	1" hardwood dowel 2' long
1 pc.	2' x 4' tempered Pegboard (hardboard with perforations)
1 box	3/4" 18-gauge wire nails
1/4 lb.	4d box nails
1 doz.	No. 10 1-1/2" flathead wood screws
1 doz.	No. 6 3/4" ovalhead screws, brass

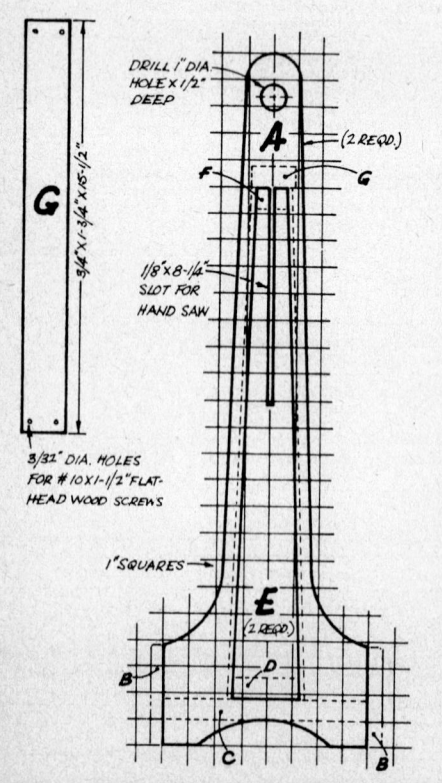

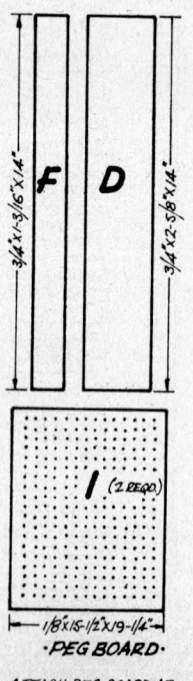

TOOL CADDY

NAIL PARTS "D", "E" & "F" FROM INSIDE USING 1-1/4" BOX NAILS

NAIL PART "C" TO PART "E" FROM BELOW

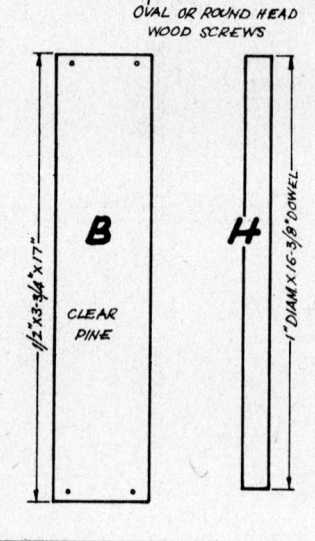

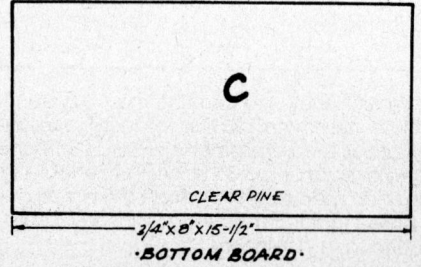

OVAL OR ROUND HEAD WOOD SCREWS

G — 3/4" x 3-3/4" x 15-1/2"

DRILL 1" DIA HOLE x 1/2" DEEP

A (2 REQD.)

1/8" x 8-1/4" SLOT FOR HAND SAW

3/32" DIA. HOLES FOR #10 x 1-1/2" FLATHEAD WOOD SCREWS

1" SQUARES

E (2 REQD)

F 3/4" x 1-3/16" x 14"
D 3/4" x 2-5/8" x 14"

I (2 REQD) — PEG BOARD — 1/8" x 15-1/2" x 19-1/4"

ATTACH PEG BOARD AT CORNERS & IN MIDDLE WITH 3/4"-18 GA. WIRE NAILS OR #6 x 3/4" ROUND HEAD WOOD SCREWS

B 1/2" x 3-3/4" x 17" CLEAR PINE

H 1" DIAM. x 16-3/8" DOWEL

C CLEAR PINE — 3/4" x 8" x 15-1/2" — BOTTOM BOARD

U-bild

HANDY HINTS FOR YOUR WORKSHOP

General-purpose and woodworking nails

Common nail: General-purpose heavy-duty type used in construction and rough work. Large head won't pull through (see detail, right).

Finishing nail: Used on trim and cabinetwork where nailheads must be concealed. Head is sunk and then filled over.

Casing nail: Similar to finishing nail but heavier. Used for trim where strength and concealment (see detail) are required.

Cut flooring nail: Has rectangular cross section and a blunt tip. Used to blind-nail flooring through edges without splitting.

Annular ring nail: Has sharp-edged ridges that lock into wood fibers and greatly increase holding power.

Spiral nails: Used in flooring to assure a tight and squeak-proof joining. Nail tends to turn into the wood like a screw as it is driven home.

Square-shank concrete nail: Similar to round types used to fasten furring strips and brackets to concrete walls and floors.

Common brads: Used for nailing parquet flooring to subfloor, attaching molding to walls and furniture. Brads are usually sunk and filled.

Tacks: Made in cut or round form; used to fasten carpet or fabric to wood, and for similar light fastening jobs.

Upholstery nails: Made with both ornamental and colored heads; used to fasten upholstery where fastenings will show.

Roofing nail: Has large head, is usually galvanized. Used to hold composition roofings; design resists pull-through.

Sealing roofing nails: Have lead or plastic washer under head to provide watertight seal; used on metal roofing.

Duplex head nail: Can be driven tight against lower head, with upper head projecting for removal; for temporary work.

Barbed dowel pin: Has many purposes, such as aligning parts, serving as pivot, permitting disassembly or separation.

Corrugated fastener: Used in making light-duty miter joints, such as in screens and large picture frames. Drive it across joint

Staples: Made in many forms to hold wire fencing, bell wire, electric cable, screening; available with insulated shoulders.

Handy Tips Courtesy of Reader's Digest

77

U-bild

Penny nail gauge

Nail sizes

Nail length is designated in inches and also by "penny" size, a term which originally related to the price per hundred, but now signifies only length. Nails are made in a wide range of lengths and types. Common nails, for example, are available in lengths from 1 inch, or 2 penny (abbreviated 2d), to 6 inches, or 60 penny.

Except in some special-purpose types, nail diameter increases with length; a 6-inch common nail is nearly four times the diameter of a 1-inch nail. Special-purpose nails, however, may come in only one size—as flooring brads do, for example—or in several lengths but only a single diameter, as some shingle nails do, depending on their purpose.

Driving nails: Nails should be driven, as a rule, through the thinner piece of wood into the thicker one, and the nail should be three times as long as the thickness of the thin piece through which it passes. Two-thirds of the nail will then be in the thicker piece for maximum holding power.

To get the best holding power from nails, drive them at angles, slanting toward or away from each other, so they cannot pull out without bending. In some cases, you can drive them through both pieces and bend (clinch) the protruding ends flat against the wood. You also get greater holding power from nails with spiral shafts or annular rings; in many, the holding power approximates the grip of screws.

Nailheads are another part of the selection story. Large heads hold best because they spread the load over a wider area, resisting pull-through. The heads of finishing nails, conversely, pull through wood quite readily. This is sometimes a welcome weakness, however, because it permits trim and cabinetwork to be disassembled by pulling through the nailheads.

Slotted **Cross-slotted** (Phillips)

right, and the **Reed & Prince**, reduce the chance of the screwdriver slipping and marring the work. Two screwdrivers will handle the usual range of Phillips screws; a single screwdriver size will drive all sizes of Reed & Prince screws.

Screws

Where to use screws

Use screws where you need greater holding power than nails can provide, and when the fastened parts may later have to be taken apart.

The most common form of screw head is the **slotted** type, left. Crossed slots, such as the **Phillips,**

Suiting the screws to the job

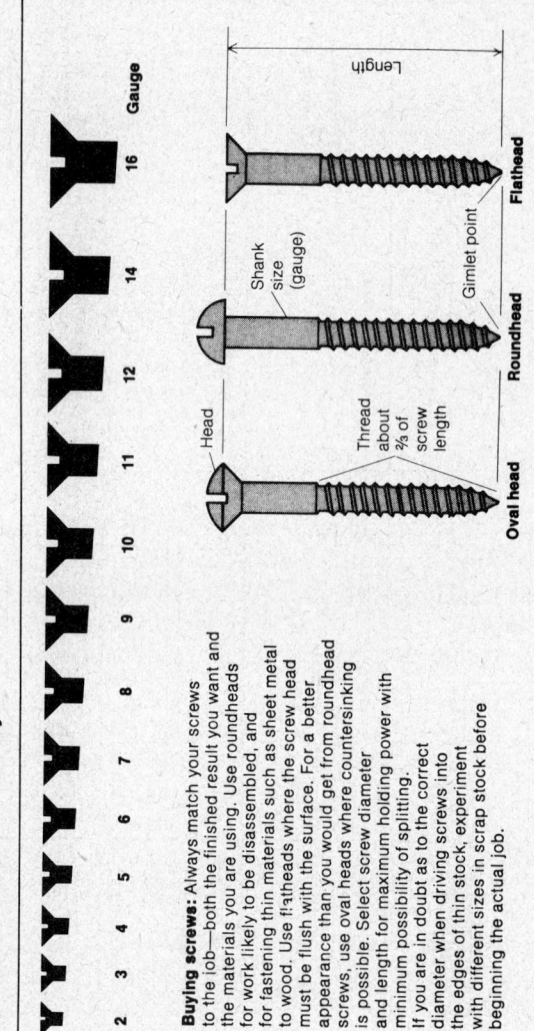

Flathead

Roundhead

Shank size (gauge)

Gimlet point

Oval head

Head

Thread about ⅔ of screw length

Length

Gauge: 2 3 4 5 6 7 8 9 10 11 12 14 16

Buying screws: Always match your screws to the job—both the finished result you want and the materials you are using. Use roundheads for work likely to be disassembled, and for fastening thin materials such as sheet metal to wood. Use flatheads where the screw head must be flush with the surface. For a better appearance than you would get from roundhead screws, use oval heads where countersinking is possible. Select screw diameter and length for maximum holding power with minimum possibility of splitting.
If you are in doubt as to the correct diameter when driving screws into the edges of thin stock, experiment with different sizes in scrap stock before beginning the actual job.

U-bild

Types of screws

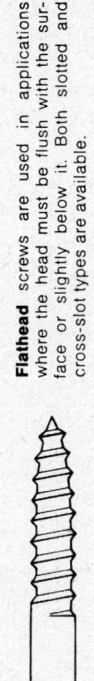

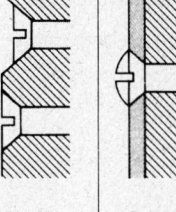

Flathead screws are used in applications where the head must be flush with the surface or slightly below it. Both slotted and cross-slot types are available.

In oval head screws, the lower portion of the head is countersunk and the top is rounded. They are easier to remove and better looking than flathead screws.

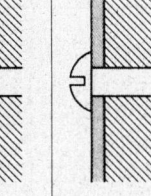

Roundhead screws are utility screws, used where the fastened piece is too thin to permit countersinking, and also on parts that may require a washer.

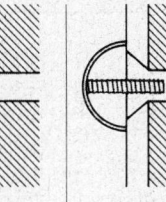

Dome head: This is a decorative form of flathead screw concealed by a dome cap. Dome heads are classed as ornamental and are available on special order only.

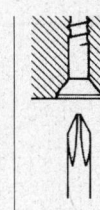

Phillips head screws have crossed slots to minimize screwdriver slip-out. Cross slots are available in most head types. A Phillips-type driver is required.

One-way screws are designed to prevent burglary and theft. If anyone should attempt to remove the screw, the screwdriver would slip out of the slot.

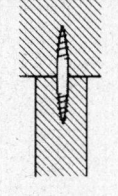

Dowel screw: This is the screw to use for end-to-end joints and similar applications unsuited to conventional screws. Usually available at large hardware outlets.

Hanger bolt (or screw) has one end that is threaded like a screw so it can be driven into wood; the other end is threaded to accept a square or a hex nut.

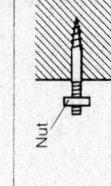

Lag bolt (or screw) is actually a heavy-duty screw and is made in sizes up to 6 in. in length. The head end is square. Bolt is driven with a wrench, as shown.

General information

Screws are preferable to nails for fastening wood. They make a tighter joint; a joint that is screwed together can be taken apart without damage. With a pilot hole, a screw will never split the wood as a nail can. When two pieces of wood are being joined with a screw, the clearance hole in the wood through which the screw first passes should pass the shank without binding. The pilot hole in the second piece should be just that—a hole into which the screw thread can bite. Without a clearance hole, the screw will not be able to draw the two pieces of wood tightly together.

Fastening with screws

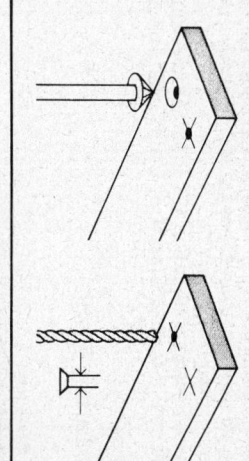

Locate and mark the screw position with intersecting lines. Hole drilled through the first piece of wood should pass shank of screw without binding.

Next, lay the bottom piece in position and mark the position of the pilot holes by using an awl. Be careful that the work does not move as you do this.

If you are using flathead screws, countersink the hole to match the diameter of the screw head. Check for right depth by dropping the screw through the hole. Fit should be flush.

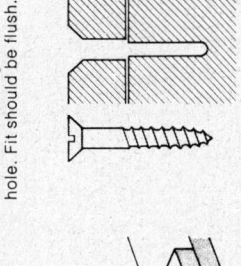

Now drill the pilot hole for the threaded part of the screw. This hole should be approximately half the depth of the length of the screw.

Handy Tips Courtesy of Reader's Digest

U-bild

Standard sizes

BOARD

1 x 2 (Actual: 3/4" x 1 1/2")
1 x 3 (Actual: 3/4" x 2 1/2")
1 x 4 (Actual: 3/4" x 3 1/2")
1 x 5 (Actual: 3/4" x 4 1/2")
1 x 6 (Actual: 3/4" x 5 1/2")
1 x 8 (Actual: 3/4" x 7 1/4")
1 x 10 (Actual: 3/4" x 9 1/4")
1 x 12 (Actual: 3/4" x 11 1/4")

DIMENSION

2 x 2 (Actual: 1 1/2" x 1 1/2")
2 x 3 (Actual: 1 1/2" x 2 1/2")
2 x 4 (Actual: 1 1/2" x 3 1/2")
2 x 6 (Actual: 1 1/2" x 5 1/2")
2 x 8 (Actual: 1 1/2" x 7 1/4")
2 x 10 (Actual: 1 1/2" x 9 1/4")
2 x 12 (Actual: 1 1/2" x 11 1/4")

3 x 4 (Actual: 2 1/2" x 3 1/2")
4 x 4 (Actual: 3 1/2" x 3 1/2")
4 x 6 (Actual: 3 1/2" x 5 1/2")
6 x 6 (Actual: 5 1/2" x 5 1/2")
8 x 8 (Actual: 7 1/2" x 7 1/2")

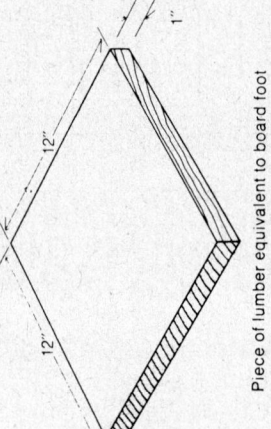

Lumber is ordered by thickness, width, and length, e.g., 2 inches x 4 inches x 8 feet. The 2-x-4 measurement refers to lumber's **nominal** dimensions (as it comes from the saw). Though the buyer orders and pays for the 2-x-4 size, the **actual** size of what he gets is 1 1/2 x 3 1/2. Standard sizes, nominal and actual, are shown. Length is as stated, not reduced by processing.

Board grades

There are two basic classifications for board lumber: (1) **Select lumber**—excellent quality, for use when appearance and ifinishing are important; and (2) **common lumber**—has defects; used for construction and general-purpose projects.

The grades of select lumber are: **B and Better grade** (or **1 and 2 clear**)—devoid of any but minute blemishes; **C select grade**—has some minor defects, such as small knots; **D select grade**—has larger imperfections which can be concealed by paint.

The corresponding select grades of Idaho White Pine are designated Supreme, Choice, and Quality.

The grades of common lumber are: **No. 1 grade**—contains tight knots, few blemishes; suitable for natural knotty finish or paint; **No. 2 grade**—has more and larger knots and blemishes; used for flooring and paneling; still suitable for knotty finish or paint; **No. 3 grade**—has loose knots and knotholes and other pronounced flaws; used for shelving, sheathing, fencing, nonvisible purposes; **No. 4 grade**—low quality; used for sheathing, subflooring, crating, and concrete forms; **No. 5 grade**—lowest board grade, for limited use where strength and appearance are not essential to the finished result.

The corresponding grades of Idaho White Pine are Colonial, Sterling, Standard, Utility, and Industrial.

Ordering wood

Board foot, the unit used in buying lumber, equals the amount of wood in a piece of lumber measuring 1 foot long, 1 inch thick, and 12 inches wide. To calculate the number of board feet, multiply length in feet by **nominal** thickness and width in inches and divide by 12. Thus, the number of board feet in a piece of lumber 6 feet long, 2 inches thick, and 6 inches wide would be:

$$\frac{6 \text{ ft.} \times 2 \text{ in.} \times 6 \text{ in.}}{12} = \frac{72}{12} = 6 \text{ board ft.}$$

Linear or running foot is the buying unit for such products as moldings, dowels, furring strips, railings, poles, sometimes 2 x 4s. Length, not thickness or width, is the only consideration. Shingles and laths are usually sold by the bundle, plywood and wallboard by the panel.

Handy Tips Courtesy of Reader's Digest

10 steps to professional wood finishing

Ever wonder how the professionals put such deep, rich and lasting finishes on the furniture they make? The answer is a matter of knowing how to apply various finishes and how to use the right sanding techniques and products to do the job with the least work and the most success, say experts at 3M Company.

1 If refinishing old furniture, remove all hardware, then take off old finish with paint and varnish remover. Follow label directions and allow to dry thoroughly. When sanding, use caution to take off as little wood as possible.

2 Be sure nails are set and joints tight, then fill all holes with wood filler or plastic wood and sand in the direction of the wood grain with fine grade sandpaper. After all scratches and old finish are removed, sand the surface to a smooth finish with extra fine grade sandpaper.

3 Clean the sanded surface with a "tack rag" or a cloth moistened with mineral spirits or turpentine to remove all sanding dust. A clean surface is vital to a professional finish in the end.

4 Begin with this step if finishing unpainted furniture. Set nails, tighten screws and check joints. Fill holes with wood filler. Sand with fine grade sandpaper, then lightly with extra fine grade sandpaper. Be sure to scuff sand all edges so stain penetrates well and finish adheres to surface. Now clean sanding dust from surface with a "tack rag" or cloth soaked in mineral spirits or turpentine.

5 STAINING: Apply stain with brush or soft cloth uniformly and in direction of grain. Cover one complete panel at a time, wiping off excess with soft cloth. Stain highlights grain and adds depth to finish. Be sure to follow manufacturer's instructions. Avoid applying stain across the grain.

6 FILLING: If the wood is porous like oak, walnut or mahogany, use a color matched paste wood filler and apply according to manufacturer's directions. When dry, sand very lightly with extra fine grade sandpaper, and clean surface with "tack rag." Since most unpainted furniture is pine or maple that does not need a filler, this can often be eliminated.

7 SEALING: Apply good quality clear wood sealer or clear wood finish over the entire surface, using brush or spray. Sealer provides flat, non-porous base for finish coats. Allow the sealer to dry thoroughly before applying second coat. If more than one coat is used, "scuff" sand lightly between coats with very fine grade sandpaper.

8 SEALER SANDING: On last sealer or primer coat, sand flat surfaces lightly to level and remove all brush or wipe marks, with very fine grade sandpaper. On other surfaces, use medium grade clean-up pad. Take extra care not to sand through sealer, and clean up with "tack rag" before finishing.

9 FINISHING: Brush on clear finish coat according to directions on label. Allow to dry thoroughly. If second coat is applied, sand first coat very lightly with extra fine sandpaper, wipe clean and brush on second coat. Having a clean surface is extremely important in this finishing step, because flecks of dust can make the difference between a professional and an amateur job. It is also very important to be sure the previous coat is dry before applying later coats, and to use care not to sand through the finish.

10 FINAL FINISH: Final sanding requires use of "wetable" sandpapers, used with rubbing oil or small amount of soapy water (use care not to let water get into glued joints). Sand in grain direction, starting at edges and working toward center, with straight strokes. For dull satin finish, use extra fine grade sandpaper with lubricant, until all bright spots on surface are gone. For medium satin finish, follow up with light sanding with super fine grade sandpaper. Apply paste wax or polish to both, and buff with soft cloth. For bright satin finish, follow above steps, but apply paste wax with fine grade clean-up pad, like "Scotch-Brite" brand, then buff with soft cloth. Final finishing is most important on tops, drawer fronts and other "eye level" parts, but it is not as crucial on other parts that might just be given a dull satin finish.

Wood types

SPECIES	CHARACTERISTICS	USES
Mahogany:	Fine-grained; reddish brown; durable; resists swelling, shrinking, and warping; easy to work	Choice cabinet wood; boat construction; plywood facings; veneers; high-grade furniture
Walnut:	Strong; fine-textured; free from warping and shrinking; easy to work; finishes well	Solid and veneered furniture; gunstocks; wall paneling; turnings; novelties; cabinetry
Oak:	Strong; durable; good bending qualities; finishes well; resists moisture absorption	Furniture; interior trim; boat frames; desks; barrels; floors; piles; handles; crossties
Maple:	Strong; hard; machines well; resists shock; fine-textured; moderate shrinkage	Flooring; fine furniture construction; wooden-ware; bowling alleys; agricultural implements
Cherry:	Close-grained; resists warping and shrinking; ages well; reddens when exposed to sunlight	Cabinetmaking; boat trim; novelties; solid furniture; handles; turned projects
Rosewood:	Very hard; dark reddish brown; close-grained; fragrant; hard to work; takes high polish	Musical instruments; piano cases; tool handles; art objects; furniture; levels; veneers
Teak:	Hard; durable; resistant to moisture and rot; resists warping, cracking, and decay	Fine furniture; paneling; shipbuilding; doors; window frames; flooring; general construction

Softwoods are susceptible, too, to very rough or split ends; allow for this by ordering 5 to 10 percent more boards than you need.

that give off a sticky liquid. These should be cleaned with turpentine, then shellac-sealed (loose knots white-glued first, then shellacked) before finishing.

SPECIES	CHARACTERISTICS	USES
Pine:	Uniform texture; works easily; finishes well; resists shrinking, swelling, and warping	House construction; paneling; trim; furniture; crates; boxes; millwork; patterns; moldings
Hemlock:	Light in weight; uniformly textured; machines well; low resistance to decay; nonresinous	Construction lumber; sheathing; doors; planks; boards; paneling; subflooring; crates
Fir:	Easily worked; finishes well; uniform texture; nonresinous; low resistance to decay	Furniture; doors; frames; windows; plywood; veneer; general millwork; interior trim
Redwood:	Light in weight; durable; easy to work; naturally resistant to decay	Outdoor furniture; fencing; house siding; interior finish; veneer; paneling
Spruce:	Strong; hard; low resistance to decay; finishes well; moderate shrinkage; light in weight	Masts and spars for ships; aircraft; crates; boxes; general millwork; ladders
Cedar:	Fresh sweet odor; reddish color; easy to work; uniform texture; resistant to decay	Chests; closet lining; shingles; posts; dock planks; novelties; Venetian blinds

Plywood grades

Most plywood made today is graded by the American Plywood Association. Look for a rubber stamp at the back or along the edges with the letters DFPA, which stand for Department For Product Approval.

The large capital letters on the grade stamp indicate the quality of the face and back: N (natural finish grade, free of defects); A (smooth and paintable, also usable for less exacting natural finish); B (allows circular repair plugs and tight knots); C (allows knotholes and splits of limited size); D (permits similar flaws, somewhat larger).

The group number indicates the species group used and relative strength ranging from Group 1, the strongest, down to Group 5. Group 1 includes, for example, plywood made from birch, Western larch, sugar maple, loblolly pine, long and short leaf pine,

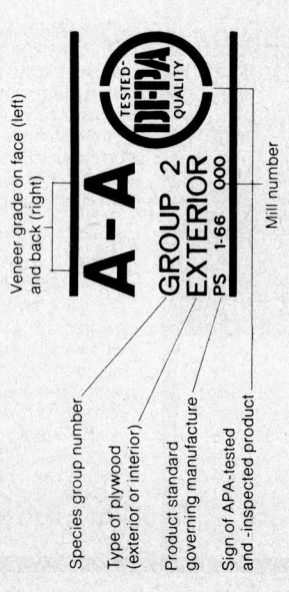

```
                        Veneer grade on face (left)
                        and back (right)

      A - A
      GROUP 2      [TESTED DFPA QUALITY]
      EXTERIOR
      PS 1-66   000
                              Mill number

Species group number
Type of plywood
(exterior or interior)
Product standard
governing manufacture
Sign of APA-tested
and -inspected product
```

and Douglas fir from Washington, Oregon, California, Idaho, British Columbia, and Alberta. Group 2 plywood is made from cedar, Western hemlock, black maple, red pine, Sitka spruce, and Douglas fir from Nevada, Utah, and New Mexico. Group 3 comprises plywood made from Alaska cedar, red alder, jack pine, lodgepole pine, Ponderosa pine, and red, white, and black spruce. Woods used in Group 4 are aspen, paper birch, Western red cedar, Eastern hemlock, sugar pine, and Engelmann spruce. Plywoods in the fifth group are made from balsam fir and poplar.

The term **Exterior** describing plywood means waterproof glue between plies; **Interior**, moisture-resistant glue, not suited to outdoor or marine use. If there are two additional numbers, such as 48/24, the first indicates maximum spacing between rafters for roof decking, the second between joists for subflooring. When the second number is zero, as 24/0, the plywood is not suitable for subflooring.

MORE "BEST-SELLER" BOOKS

#U110 TRACEABLE & FANCIFUL FABRIC FRAMES $4.50
This 24-page color-illustrated guidebook includes step-by-step photos and instructions, traceable patterns, complete materials lists, and handy hints for creating 14 stylish frames.

#GM37 CANVASING THE BACKROADS $6.25
You can create beautiful oil paintings just by following the simple directions in this 34-page guidebook. Traceable patterns are from photographs taken around the country. 10 patterns in all.

#GM42 SOFT SCULPTURE FOR ALL SEASONS $4.25
Start saving your old stockings and transform them into year-round conversation pieces. This colorful 23-page instruction guide contains 18 different projects for all seasons.

#M801 PUFFY PEOPLE $3.50
This 15-page booklet contains 14 different projects such as Doctor Dilly, George Washington, a whistling fisherman, cuddly babies, a toothful witch, pigs in the cornfield and more. Included are helpful hints and basic stitching directions.

#J110 CROCHETED ORIGINALS & FAVORITES VOL. 6 $4.75
This is the latest addition to the popular Jessie Abularach collection of original crochet patterns. 30 different projects are all in this 23-page guidebook.

#L105 THE BITSY KIDS $5.25
The Bitsy Kids are soft, cuddly dolls a child can hug, love and play with, without worry of breaking or soiling. Tess and Rusty, as well as their clothing, are all washable and their unique construction makes them smoother and softer than most cloth dolls. Each one stands approx. 25" high. The 14-page guidebook has full-size traceable patterns for doll bodies and clothes.

#G465 BABY BOUTIQUE $7.25
From bibs to bumper pads...here is everything you need to welcome that new-born bundle of joy. Over 17 projects are included in this full-color 33-page guidebook. A cozy bunting, crib toys, stroller bag, baby seat cover, tote bag and a crib ensemble are just some of the items offered.

#L104 FABRIC MICE $5.25
These fuzzy fabric mice are the only kind you'll want in your home. Mr. and Mrs. Doorstop Mouse will quietly sit by your door, and Itty Bitty Mouse loves to poke his nose in everything. Handy hints tell you how to create beards, curl hair and other finishing touches. 14-page guidebook.

#SP36 NOSTALGIC CROCHET $4.25
These simple crochet patterns take on a touch of Victorian elegance when combined with ribbons, fabric and silk flowers. 29 different projects are included in this 15-page guidebook, each with its own materials list and step-by-step directions. Also offered are full-size traceable patterns, charts and crochet basics and techniques.

#SP31 FOLDING WITH QUILTED STAR $4.25
The most popular patchwork design, and a long-time favorite of quilters, is the star. This 15-page guidebook uses a quick-folding technique which produces the same effect our great-grandmothers obtained when stitching each piece by hand. Full-size traceable patterns help you create placemats, potholders, appliance covers, wall decor, and more.

#FM7 CHILDREN'S TOYS AND FURNITURE $7.50
A beautiful 160-page book featuring 50 step-by-step projects. Toy chests, puzzles, riding toys, cradles, tables and chairs, plus more. Each project has a complete materials list, and exploded drawing, scaled pattern pieces, photos and written instructions. Also included is a section on tools and materials, as well as a glossary of terms.

#584 TELL IT-MAKE IT BOOK $4.50
Looking for a way to keep the kids away from the television set? Well, Shari Lewis, with her puppet Lambchop, have created this 112-page, hard-cover book of stories and crafts for children ages 5 through 12 years. They'll be able to choose from a variety of 60 projects.

#SD4 THE STROM TOYS $9.95
This delightfully illustrated book tells the story of why the little Stroms helped the authors make toys for their grandchildren's Christmas and how they overcome their worst enemy. 40 designs for which plans can be ordered are included: 10 construction toys, 13 boats, 3 rocking horses, 4 puzzles, 1 wagon and lots more. Mini-plans included with book.

ALL PRICES INCLUDE POSTAGE. USE ORDER FORMS IN BACK OF CATALOG.

More Ways to $AVE
(discounted plans & books)

#C26 Hutch Packet $5.40
Includes Welsh Cabinet, Corner Cabinet, Dutch Buffet, Buffet/Hutch.

#C27 Handicraft Grab Bag $5.00
Fantasy Bead Trees, Hardware Sculpture, Arrange Flowers, Latch Hook, Weaving, Bread Dough.

#C28 Handicraft Grab Bag $5.00
Latch Hook, Fiber Flowers, String Art, Chenille, Bead & Pearl Jewelry, Furry Novelties.

#C29 Sewing Cabinets $6.00
Cabinets, Tables, Mending Bench.

#C31 Chair Combination $4.00
California Lawn Chair, Redwood Lawn Chair, Director's Chair.

#C35 Holiday Packet $7.00
Christmas Train, Small Resurrection, Santa's Head, Merry Christmas Sign & more.

#C40 Bedroom Storage $4.00
Silent Valet, Bed Desk, Trouser Rack, Under-Bed-Storage, Portable Wardrobe.

#C42 Lamp Packet $4.00
Boudoir Lamp, Table Lamp, Bedside Lamp, Swag Lamp, Decorator Lamp.

#C54 Audiophile Packet $6.00
Stereo Cabinet, Record Cabinet/Bookcase, Home Entertainment Center, Liquor Cabinet/Stereo Center, Tape Storage Units.

#C59 Coffee Table Combo $10.00
Hatch Cover, Display Case, Parquet, Butler's and Game style tables.

#CB14 Sewing Grab Bag $9.95
Embroidery, Fabric Yo-Yo's, Applique, Country Patchwork, Pocket Pillows, Ribbons & Trims.

#CB17 Craft Book Grab Bag $9.95
Chenille, Craft Sticks, Calico Patch Painting, Book-A-Page, Beading Brilliance, Wall Plaques.

U-Bild Grab Bag Specials
(add postage from chart on page 112)

A. Oak Furniture Classics (#C55)
This classic collection includes three popular antique oak reproductions. The lawyer's bookcase is stackable...you choose whether it's 2, 3 or 4 shelves high. An oak file cabinet which will even hold legal-size hanging files. And the third member is the old-favorite oak ice box. Retail Value—$9.00
Special—$5.75

B. Bedroom Set (#C56)
Your bedroom can look like new with this 6-piece suite in country pine. Included are dresser, mirror, nightstand, headboard, chest-on-chest and armoire. Build the complete set or individual pieces and stain to match your own furniture. Retail Value—$12.00
Special—$8.00

C. Cradle Packet (#C32)
Four stylish cradles for that special little someone. The heritage cradle shown here features a hood and rests on the floor. Raised on a pedestal with spindle sides is the country-style cradle. Packet includes two more. Retail Value—$12.00
Special—$6.00

D. Train 'N Truck Packet (#C53)
Three foot-powered vehicles for kids to enjoy up and down their street. Each plan includes step-by-step instructions and photos, plus full-size traceable pieces wherever possible. A mail truck (pictured), a diesel truck and a locomotive. Retail Value—$9.00
Special—$4.00

E. PVC Furniture Packet (#C25)
Outdoor furniture made from PVC pipe is durable and stylish. This group includes lounge furniture, a dining set, lawnswing and hammock. PVC pipe is available in most home centers or plumbing supply stores. Retail Value—$12.00 **Special—$6.00**

F. Headboard Packet (#C24)
This collection of bed and bedroom furniture will appeal to the young and the old alike. Several different headboards, a bedroom console (shown here), and a combination chest-bed-bookcase are included. Retail Value—$9.00 **Special—$5.00**

THIS 'N' THAT

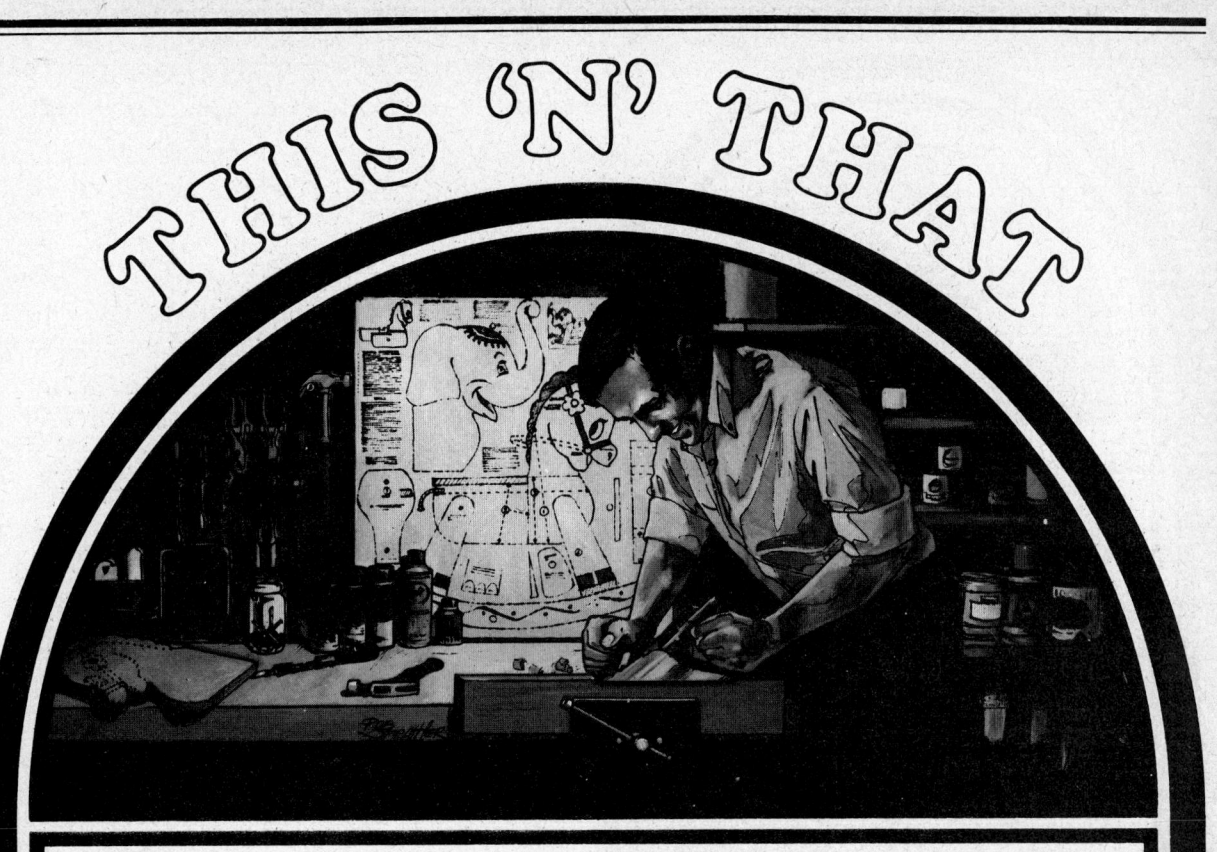

Item	Page	Item	Page
Awnings	87	Knick-Knack Shelves	91, 110
Bargain Packets	105	Lamps	94, 110
Bars & Stools	94, 104	Lawn Chairs	88, 94
Beds	110	Lawn Ornaments	87
Benches	93	Leaf Bagger	88
Bird Houses	86, 87	Leathercraft	89
Boats	103	Letters & Numerals	89
Bookends	89, 108	Macrame	101
Bookshelves	93	Mail Box Holder	87
Buffet	90	Miniatures	89
Card Tables	110	Mirrors	104
Centerpieces	102	Murals	100, 101
Chairs	94, 104	Outdoor Storage	95, 106
Chaise Lounges	88, 106	Outdoor Camping	109
Christmas Displays (color)	96, 97, 98, 99	Parts Rack	89
Christmas Displays (paint-yourself)	98, 99	Pet Items	108, 109
Christmas Ornaments	101	Plant Care Books	106
Clocks	94, 95	Playhouses	107
Closets	92	Pool Tables	103
Coffee Tables	90	Safety Pin Jewelry	89
Cold Frame	88	Sewing Cabinets	94
Concrete Patio	88	Scrapbook	89
Craft Sticks	89	Shoe Bar	92
Cue Rack	103	Silent Valet	92
Decoupage	89	Shopping Cart	110
Den	104	Shuffleboard	103
Desks	90, 93, 94, 104, 107	Stitchery Crafts	89, 101
Dining Sets	86, 90, 104, 106, 110	String Art	101, 110
Dressing Table	92	Sun Tanner	86
End Tables	90, 93, 95, 103, 104	Storage Chests	90, 92, 104, 108, 110
Exercise Equipment	103	Telephone Cover-Up	104
Feather Jewelry	89	Toys	107, 108
Fences	103	TV Cabinets	93
Fireplace	104	Wall Hangings	100
Folding Screen	104	Wardrobes	92, 104
Game Tables	103	Weathervanes	86
Headboards	92	Window Box & Shutters	87
Horse Racing Game	103	Workbench	89
Junk Art	89		

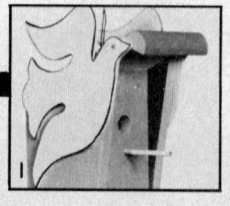

A. Garden Settee (#396)
An outdoor loveseat for two — approx. 22" x 46". **$2.75**

B. Potting Bench (#425)
Operating Table for plant surgeons.

C. Weathervane (#151)
Full-size traceable patterns for the mule and hobo. **$1.00**

D. Weathervane (#152)
As the breeze blows, the pianist plays. **$1.00**

E-J. Bird Shelters & Feeders (#684)
Step-by-step directions for all 6 models. **$2.50**

K. Bird House Assortment (#C12)
7 homes for our fine feathered friends. **$4.00**

L-M. Robin Shelters (#146)
Step-by-step instructions make these a cinch. **$1.00**

N. Wren House (#71)
A simple-to-build project for any amateur. **$1.00**

A. Lawn Ornaments (#3)
7 cutouts include a rooster, calf, 2 dogs, & more. $2.00

B. Lawn Ornaments (#14)
6 quick-and-easy animal cutouts. Trace/cut/paint. **$3.00**

C. Bird Feeder (#341)
Turn your backyard into a bird paradise! $1.00

D. Window Box (#160)
Or use as a shelf to hold flower pots. $1.00

E. Door & Window Awnings (#259324)
Ventilated, slat-style awnings keep you cool. $1.50

F. Uncle Sam Mailbox Holder (#529)
Also a flag stand! Life-size character. $1.00

G. Shutters (#674)
Patterns include a tulip, heart, boat & girl. $2.00

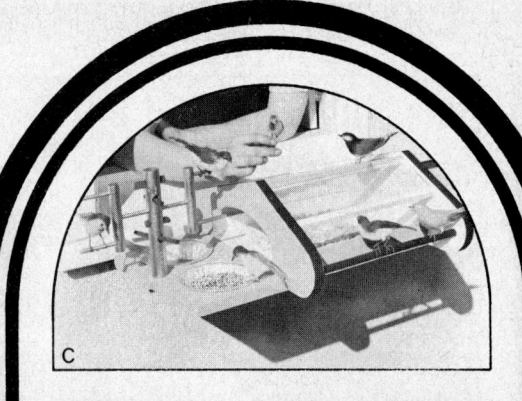

87

A. **Comfo-Chaise** (#93)
Elevates your feet. **$1.00**

B. **Outdoor Chaise** (#81)
Adjustable back. **$1.50**

C. **Double Chaise** (#182)
Standard-size pads. **$1.50**

D. **Easy-Rest Chaise** (#125)
Glides over lawns. **$1.00**

E. **Summer Furniture** (#688)
Folds up... portable! **$2.00**

F. **Slant Chaise** (#322)
Sunbathe or exercise. **$1.00**

G. **Reclining Chair** (#111)
Canvas & wood frame. **$1.00**

H. **Hostess Chair** (#116)
Economy & comfort. **$1.00**

I. **Concrete Patio** (#514)
Do-it-yourself. **$2.00**

J. **Sun-Sauna Lounge** (#499)
Tan & Relax! **$1.00**

K. **Low-Down Chair** (#202)
Perfect for beach. **$1.00**

L. **Cold Frame** (#444)
Mini hot house. **$1.00**

M. **Leaf Bagger** (#493)
Uses plastic bags. **$1.00**

A. Men's Belt (#187)
Made from leather. $1.00

A. Women's Belt (#188)
Easy-to-make. $1.00

B. Wallet (#185)
Follow a pattern. $1.00

B. Purse (#186)
Handsome styling. $1.00

C. Holster (#184)
Perfect gift. $1.00

D. Leather Craft (#531)
Clever selection. $2.00

E. Book Ends (#124)
Cute calves. $1.00

F. Photo Album (#69)
Save the memories. $1.00

G. Letters & Nos. (#66)
For your home. $1.00

H. Parts Rack (#64)
It revolves! $1.00

I. Workbench (#92)
Easy-to-build. $1.00

J. Window Valence (#61)
A decorator touch. $1.00

K. Safety-pin Jewelry (#566)
Stylish & clever. $1.50

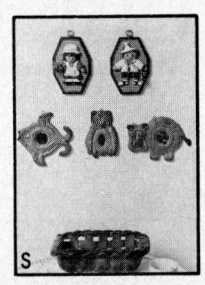

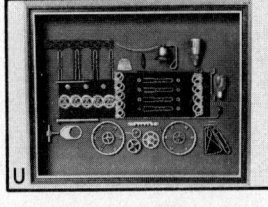

L. No-Sew Patchwork (#585)
Mansion measures 21" x 27". $2.00

M. Snip N' Stick (#523)
Fake stitchery. $2.00

N. Hishi-Feather Macrame (#HA49)
Learn to make jewelry. $1.50

O. Craft Sticks (#611)
Easy-to-make planters. $2.00

P. Redwood Chair (#602)
This handsome chair is a cinch!

Q. Decoupage (#495)
"Frame" pics on plaques. $2.00

R. Resined Plaque (#533)
A glass-like finish. $2.00

S. Bread Dough (#561)
Flour, salt & water. $2.00

T. Purse & Print Decoupage (#541)
Step-by-step directions. $2.00

U. Junk Art (#545)
Use common junk items. $2.00

V. Miniature Rooms (#HH10)
Scale cut-outs included. $2.50

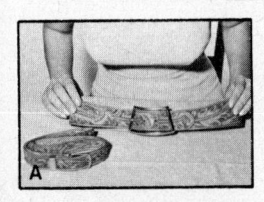

89

E. Buffet (#412)
Step-by-step plan.
63"l x 30"w x 32"h. $1.50

F. Kitchen Island (#326)
Extra storage room.
36" x 44." $2.00

G. Planter (#274)
Designed for indoor or outdoor use.

A. Breakfast Nook (#220)
Bench storage. $1.00

B. Dining Set (#301339)
Drop-leaf style. $2.00

C. Dining Set (#347378)
Table & Chairs. $2.00

D. Hi-Lo Table (#314)
Up to 5' long. $1.00

H. Coffee Table (#105)
Strong and durable.
Easy-to-build. $1.00

I. Coffee Table (#275)
Also a storage chest.
18"x16"x48" long. $1.50

J. Cocktail Table (#306)
Sliding top sections are removable. $1.00

K. Harem Set (#252)
Table & chairs. $1.00

L. Cocktail Table (#393)
Revolving rack. $1.00

M. Desk (#157)
A necessity! $1.00

N. Storage Chest (#198)
Versatile. $1.00

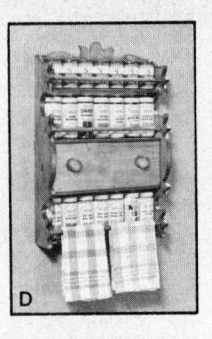

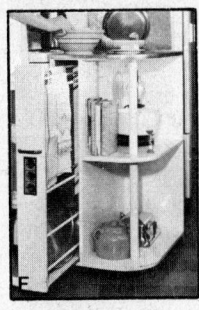

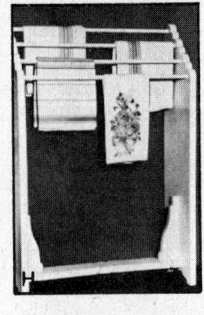

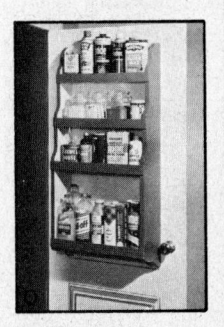

A. Utility Shelf (#63)
Spices too! $1.00

B. Kitchen Shelf (#221)
Revolves. $1.00

C. Chef's Cart (#204)
Or a portable bar

D. Spice Shelf (#269)
Quaint style. $1.00

E. Wall Shelf (#222)
Knick-knacks. $1.00

F. Kitchen Unit (#65)
Stores it all! $2.00

G. Wall Cabinet (#365)
Handy & easy! $1.00

H. Towel Rack (#70)
Bath or kitchen. $1.00

I. Phone Shelf (#215)
Easy-to-do. $1.00

J. Kitchen Dolly (#277)
On casters. $1.00

K. Bookcase (#205)
Quick & easy. $1.00

L. Vegetable Bin (#234)
Self-stacking. $1.00

M. Shelf (#68)
Collectibles. $1.00

N. Dispenser (#325)
Wax paper, etc. $1.00

O. Door Shelf (#171)
Convenient. $1.00

P. What-Not Shelf (#58)
Odds and ends. $1.00

Q. Spice Shelf (#404)
Made of plywood. $1.00

R. Wall Shelf (#67)
Displays china. $1.00

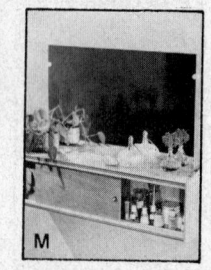

A. **Headboard (#357)**
Elegant lines. $1.00

A. **Boudoir Lamp (#359)**
Read in bed. $1.00

A. **Nitestand (#360)**
Easy-to-do. $1.00

B. **Headboard (#427)**
Any size bed. $1.00

C. **Jungle Gym Bed (#542)**
Store toys in its base. $2.75

D. **Hexagonal Table (#414)**
Roomy storage area, 15" high. $2.75

E. **Chifforobe (#337)**
6 drawers. $1.50

F. **T.V. Cabinet (#622)**
Make any T.V. a console.

G. **Silent Valet (#148)**
Handy & neat. $1.00

H. **Hamper (#273)**
Ventilated. $1.00

I. **Shoe Rack (#110)**
Any length. $1.00

J. **Hat/Coat Rack (#88)**
Hang it all! $1.00

K. **Trouser Rack (#460)**
Trim & Tidy. $1.00

L. **Bedside Table (#344)**
Swingout tray. $1.00

M. **Wall Cabinet (#216)**
Versatile! $1.00

N. **Storage Chest (#462)**
Under-the-bed. $1.00

O. **Dressing Table (#482)**
Lift-up mirror. $1.00

P. **Bunk Beds (#354)**
Trace & saw. $2.00

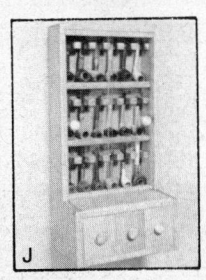

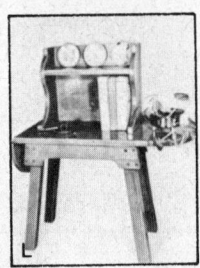

A. **Wall Unit (#346)**
8' tall. $2.00

B. **Deacon Bench (#390)**
Occasional bench. $1.00

C. **Corner Desk (#489)**
4-piece set. $2.00

D. **Library (#135)**
Corner-perfect. $1.00

E. **Window Valence (#115)**
Dress-up decor. $1.00

F. **TV Cabinet (#367)**
Or liquor cabinet $1.50

G. **TV Cart (#219)**
Easy-to-build. $1.00

H. **Record File (#214)**
Neat & orderly. $1.00

I. **Cabinet (#128)**
Multi-purpose. $1.00

J. **Pipe Cabinet (#270)**
Holds 18 pipes. $1.00

K. **Smoker (#57)**
Quick & easy! $1.00

L. **Dropleaf Table (#72)**
Monterey-style. $1.00

M. **Corner Cabinet (#109)**
Handsome piece. $1.00

N. **Handy Cabinet (#420)**
For small items. $1.00

N. **Mending Bench (#422)**
Easy-to-build. $1.00

O. **Woodbasket (#78)**
Convenient. $1.00

O. **Fireside Bench (#79)**
Or coffee table. $1.00

P. **Paper Baler (#246)**
Neat bundles. $1.00

$3.00 ... ALL PATTERN PRICES ARE $3.00 UNLESS OTHERWISE MARKED
(Plus postage — see chart on page 112)

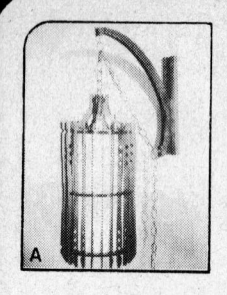

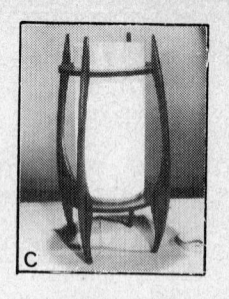

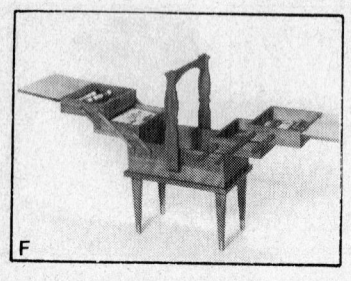

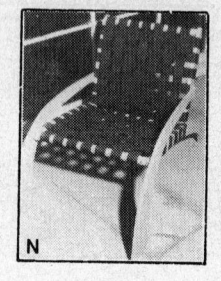

A. Swag Lamp (#402)
Hang in any room. $1.00

B. Table Lamp (#356)
Simple-to-do. $1.00

C. Boudoir Lamp (#304)
Fiberglass shade. $1.00

D. Decorator Lamp (#437)
Table top or wall. $1.00

E. Phone Stand (#199)
Easily-built. $1.00

F. Sewing Cabinet (#253)
Folds up. $1.00

G. Sewing Cabinet (#272)
Stores machine. $1.00

H. End Table Desk (#303)
Top opens. $1.00

I. Hanging Desk (#176)
28"lx20"hx8"deep. $1.00

J. Mantle Clock (#477)
Uses battery. $1.00

K. Rocking Chair (#345)
Full-size pattern. $1.50

K. Foot Rest (#476)
For sore feet. $1.00

L. Kibitzer Chair (#86)
Trace & saw. $1.00

M. Lawn Rocker (#130)
Perennial favorite. $1.50

N. Chair (#106)
Quick & easy. $1.00

O. Stool (#126)
Details given. $1.00

P. Bar Stool (#133)
Solid styling. $1.00

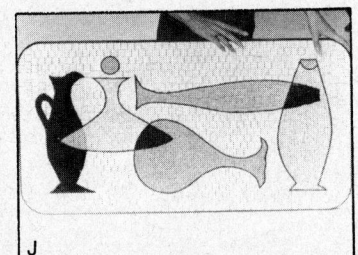

A. **Sports Corner (#497)**
Storage area. $2.00
B. **Desk Workbench (#498)**
Lift desk top. $1.00
C. **Sewing Box (#195)**
Holds all! $1.00
D. **Bookcase (#77)**
Quick & easy. $1.00
E. **Record Cabinet (#166)**
Sized for albums. $1.00

F. **Room Divider (#225)**
Use two sides or one.
G. **Coaster Set (#104)**
Colorful & easy. $1.00
H. **Lazy Susan (#132)**
Useful item. $1.00
I. **Parsons Tables (#503)**
Set of 3 on one pattern.
J. **Mosaic Tables (#C-8)**
8 designs. $6.00
K. **Foot Rest (#158)**
Folds away. $1.00

L. **Shoe Shine Box (#127)**
Easy-to-do. $1.00
M. **Cabinet (#247)**
Multi-purpose. $1.00
N. **Corner Cabinet (#426)**
Stands 6 feet high.
O. **Magazine Rack (#108)**
Wall style. $1.00
P. **Decorator Clocks (#468)**
3 styles. $1.00

A. Little Drummer Boy (#509)
Full-color & printed on weather-resistant paper. Just glue onto plywood, cut out, and he comes to life on your front lawn 42"x58". **$7.50**

B. Five Elves (#10)
Full-color on weather-resistant paper...just glue onto wood and cut out. **$7.50** Santa's Helper Sign (#297) **50¢**

C. Toy Soldier (#740)
This rosy-cheeked sentry stands 4½' tall. Full-color poster. **$7.50**

D. Nativity Scene (#7)
⅔ lifesize. Full color & weather-resistant. Just glue onto plywood, cut out and stand up. "Come let us adore him.". **$18.00**

96

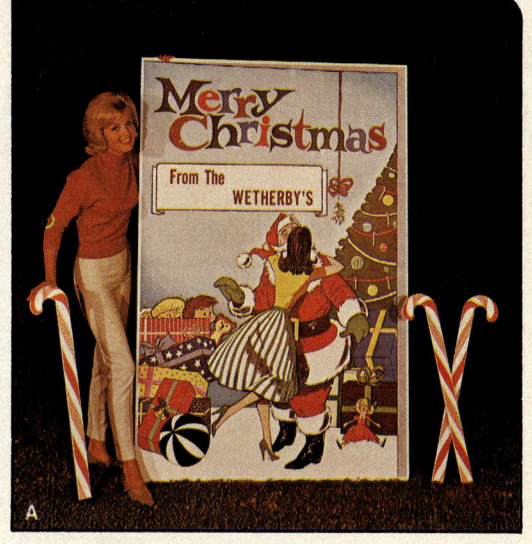

A. Giant Christmas Card (Poster #296)
6' high and 4' wide. Just glue the waterproof poster onto plywood and display. **$4.00**
Candy Canes (#292) $2.00 per dozen.

B. Carolers (#510)
Depicting a family in the Old English tradition of caroling. This full-color scene measures 76" x 52" and is printed on weather-resistant paper. **$7.50**

C. Snow Family (#C6)
Full-color posters on heavy weather-resistant paper. Snowman (#218) **$4.50**; Mrs. Snowman (#226) **$4.50**; Snow Kids (#227) **$4.00**. Or order all together for **$13.00**.

D. Santa, Sleigh & Reindeer (#C20)
Super outdoor display. Santa (#189) **$4.00**; Mrs. Santa (#335) **$4.00**; Sleigh (#257) **$7.00**; 8 Reindeer (#256) **$10.00**. Or order all together for **$24.00** (save $1.00). All posters in the #C20 group are printed in color, ready to glue to plywood, and saw out.

COLOR DECORATIONS

A. Season's Greetings Decoration (#295) $2.00
B. "Christmas Whimsies" Set (#589) $8.00 (not color)
C. Angel Decorations (#258) $2.00 each
C. Candles (#293) $2.00 per dozen
C. Merry Christmas Sign (#298) $.50
D. Myron the Christmas Mouse (#536) $3.00
E. Easter Bunny (#447) $1.00 (not color)
E. Resurrection (#9) $1.00
F. Three Wise Men (#327)
   4' x 6' color poster. $4.00
G. Santa's Christmas Train (#5) $3.00 (not color)
H. Santa, Sleigh & Deer (#4) $2.50 (not color)

  * Projects marked "not color" are paint-by-number.

COLOR DECORATIONS
A. The Red-Nosed Reindeer (#554) $3.00
B. Choir Boy and Angel (#153) $1.00
C. Miniature Nativity Scene (#17918O) $2.00
D. Five Elves (#10) **$7.50**
D. Santa's Helpers Sign (#297) 50c
E. Resurrection Figure (#191) $2.00
F. Santa's Head (#183) $1.50
F. Stocking (#294) $2.00
G. Gingerbread House (#591). $2.00

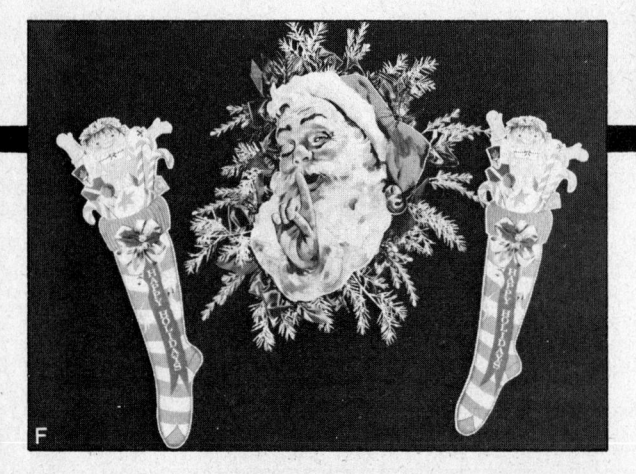

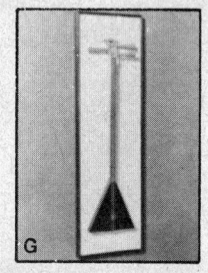

A. **Color Mural (#355)**
Hang or frame it. **$5.00**

B. **Monterey Pine (#308)**
Paint yourself. **$2.00**

C. **Lake Scene (#331)**
10'w x 3'h. **$2.00**

D. **Pictures (#2)**
Five duets. **$2.00**

E. **Gag Pictures (#13)**
Saw & paint. **$3.00**

F. **String Yachts (#452)**
Colored yarn. **$1.00**

G. **Balalaika (#415)**
Easy-to-do. **$1.00**

H. **Flower Bouquet (#317)**
28"w x 3'h. **$1.00**

I. **Lion Tapestry (#400)**
Felt & yarn. **$1.00**

J. **String Picture (#413)**
Geometric form. **$1.50**

K. **Mural Designs (#11)**
For window shades. **$1.50**

L. **Pig Cut-Outs (#321)**
20" x 20" each. **$1.00**

M. **Marine Plaque (#416)**
Eye-catching! **$1.00**

- **A. New Macrame (#H450)**
  32-page book. $3.00
- **B. More Macrame (#H452)**
  Color photos. $3.00
- **C. Plywood Plant (#516)**
  Trace, cut & paint. $1.00
- **D. Balloon Mural (#505)**
  Yarn & nails. $1.00
- **E. Lil' Sergeant (#506)**
  18" x 30" picture. $1.50
- **F. Owl (#496)**
  Full-size pattern. $1.50
- **G. Macrame (#547)**
  Belts & hangers. $2.00
- **H. Sunburst (#544)**
  20" x 24". $1.00
- **I. Sailboat Plaque (#527)**
  Brass nails & string. $1.50
- **J. Basic Basketry (#GM5)**
  Coiling & twining. $2.50
- **K. Silk Flowers (#HA48)**
  Exotic-looking! $1.50
- **L. Critter Pillows (#643)**
  Latch hook. $2.00
- **M. Rug Tapestry (#600)**
  Scraps & glue. $1.50
- **N. Wreaths (#568)**
  For Christmas! $2.00
- **O. 3 Kings & Angel (#567)**
  12"-15" tall. $2.00
- **P. Dough Ornaments (#590)**
  12 in all. $2.00
- **Q. 3-D String Art (#HA31)**
  Easy & fun! $2.00
- **R. Street Scene (#379)**
  9' mural. $3.00
- **S. Lake-of-the Woods (#501)**
  Trace & paint mural. $2.00
- **T. Sheep (#548)**
  Coiled string. $1.00

101

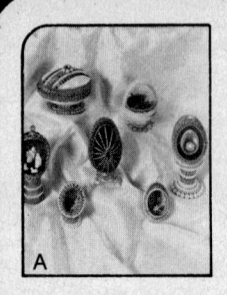

A. **Egg Decorating** (#524)
   Ornaments too! $1.50
B. **Card Castle** (#441)
   Unique decor. $1.00
C. **Centerpiece** (#278)
   Valentine's Day. $1.00
D. **Centerpiece** (#290)
   Baby shower. $1.00
E. **Centerpiece** (#289)
   Wedding shower. $1.00
F. **Sugar Church** (#271)
   Glue & cubes. $1.00
G. **Sugar Castle** (#249)
   A magic idea! $1.00
H. **Centerpiece** (#282)
   Cart & donkey. $1.00
I. **Candle Maker** (#521)
   Create your own. $2.00
J. **Tissue Boxes.** (#487)
   Decoupaged. $1.00
K. **Candy Cottage** (#438)
   Yummy! $1.00
L. **Six Candles** (#386)
   For Holidays. $1.00
M. **Easel** (#463)
   And paint box. $1.50
N. **Scatter Pins** (#107)
   Zodiac signs. $1.00
O. **Centerpiece** (#114)
   Sleigh $1.00

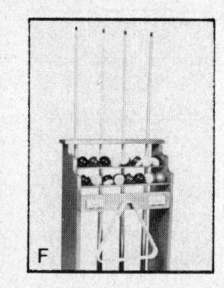

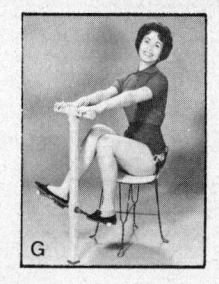

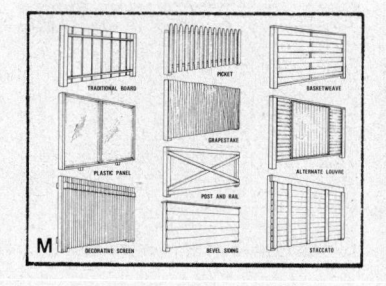

A. Junior Pool Table (#459)
Easy-to-do. $1.50

B. Table Tennis (#123)
Fun for all! $1.00

C. Horse Racing Game (#453)
Rules included. $1.00

D. Colonial End Table (#75)
Collector's item. $1.00

E. Shuffleboard (#155)
3 court sizes. $1.00

F. Cue Rack (#443)
Stores billiard equipment. $1.00

G. Cycle Exerciser (#203)
Firm up those muscles and feel good! $1.00

H. Aqua Board (#240)
Easier to ride than skis. $1.00

I. 16 Foot Boat (#175)
Designed for speed and power. $2.00

J. Cabin Cruiser (#194)
18 Ft. $2.00

K. 11-1/2 Ft. Skiff (#147)
Motor or row. $2.00

L. Exercise Board (#156)
Trim up! $1.00

M. Ten Fences (#551)
Easy-to-do. $2.00

N. Family Gym (#287)
Made of pipe. $1.00

103

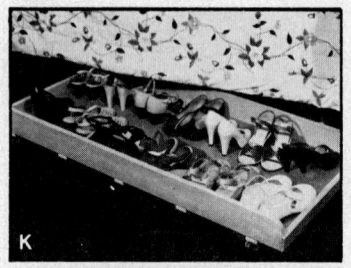

A. Wardrobe (#483)
Easy-to-build closet. **$2.00**

B. Closet Conversion (#311)
Holds a TV set. **$2.00**

C. Wardrobe (#629)
12 cubic ft. of storage. **$2.00**

D. Telephone Cover-Up (#676)
Incl. foldup wall desk.

E. Magazine End Table (#434)
Holds 100 magazines. **$2.00**

F. Portable Bar (#197)
Glides on casters. **$1.00**

G. Director's Chair (#605)
Conveniently folds up. **$2.00**

I. Breakfast Nook (#333)
Colonial style. **$2.00**

J. Mirror Set (#660)
For every bedroom. **$1.50**

L. All-Purpose Den (#492)
Entertainment center. **$2.00**

M. Holiday Fireplace (#687)
Store after holidays. **$2.00**

N. Decorator Screen (#656)
Great room divider. **$1.00**

H-K. Bed Desk (#677)
Incl. under-bed storage tray. **$1.50**

More Ways To $AVE

#C18 HANDICRAFTS $7.50
Chenille Circus, Basic Basketry, Critter Pillows, String Art, Zodiac Signs and Americana Weaving.

#C19 Kiddie Furniture $5.00
Robot Dresser, Step Chair, Table and Chair, Rocker, Froggy High Chair.

#C23 Lawn & Garden Packet $5.00
Comfo Chaise, Bird Shelters, Pergola, Trash Container, Storage Shed, Wishing Well.

#C34 SHELF PACKET $4.00
Spice Shelves, Back-of-Door Shelf, Revolving Wall Shelves.

#C36 DESK PACKET $5.00
Modern, Hanging, Office, Trestle, Mini-Rolltop and Pull-Down styles.

#C38 CLOCK PACKET $5.00
Wall, Decorator, Mantle, Pendulum, and Grandfather styles.

#C41 PHYSICAL FITNESS $5.00
Exercise Slantboard, Exerciser, Jogger, Row-er-ciser.

#C46 SPORTS PACKET $4.00
Gun Racks, Sportsman's Corner, Camper-Boat-Cartop Carrier.

#C47 GAME PACKET $4.00
Shuffleboard, Ping Pong Table, Cue Rack, Horse Racing Game, Jr. Pool Table, Bumper Pool Table.

#C48 BUNK BED PACKET $4.00
Cablecar, Del Mar Bunk and Newport Bunk styles.

#C49 PLAYHOUSE PACKET $4.00
Fort-style, 4'x4' Playhouse, A-Frame.

#C50 PATIO PACKET $5.00
Brick Patio, Block Wall, Decking, Patio Storage, Patio Cover, Carport.

#C51 OUTING PACKET $4.00
Travel Aid, Car-Top Kitchen, Picnic Desk, Car Trailer, Car Bike Rack, Camper.

#C52 BOOKCASES $4.00
Room Divider, Pocket-Book Shelf, Caravan Storage Wall, Grow-Light Bookcase.

U-Bild Grab Bag Specials
(add postage from chart on page 112)

A. Greenthumb Grab Bag (#C43)
This special selection of easy-to-follow plans and patterns can turn your brown thumb green. Different projects include a guidebook on ferns; lean-to and standard greenhouses; a storage barn (6'x8'); a potting bench; redwood planters; and more.
Retail Value – $26.00 **Special – $9.50**

B. Handicraft Bonanza (#C-37 & #C-30)
#C-37 is a special selection of 5 plans for craft projects. Lion tapestry & others.
Retail Value – $6.00 **Special – $4.50**
#C-30 is a macrame packet featuring five instruction guides with dozens of simple projects.
Retail Value – $11.50 **Special – $7.00**

C. Toy Spectacular (#C33)
With the price of toys going sky-high, now is the time to build some simple, safe wooden toys. Plans include animal pull toys; a pony to ride and others to entertain young ones for hours.
Retail Value – $9.00 **Special – $4.00**

D. Mural Madness (#C-45)
Now, you can add to the beauty of your home with this handy set of 3 custom murals for your walls. Trace these patterns on the wall and follow the paint-by-numbers method. Lake-of-the-Woods; Mountain Lake; and Flower Bouquet. Includes color charts.
Retail Value – $5.00 **Special – $3.00**

E. Home Improvement Package (#C-44)
With this special packet you can add dollar value to your home. Five step-by-step plans include complete room addition; how to lay a brick patio; complete guide on paneling a room; and an easy-to-follow plan for building a patio cover.
Retail Value – $14.50 **Special – $6.50**

F. Summer Savings (#C-22)
Anytime is a good time to build these outdoor projects. Special package includes patterns and plans for 9 useful outdoor items: Birdshelters; barbecue table; outdoor glider swing; bird feeder; window box; trash-container and more!
Retail Value – $12.00 **Special – $5.00**

A. Storage Center (#513)
This outdoor structure measures 8½' tall x 8' wide. **$1.00**

B. Mother Nature's Secrets (#H600)
Answers all questions about house plants. **$4.00**

C. Trash Bin (#340)
Keep dogs and cats out of trash or store firewood. **$1.00**

D-F. 3-in-1 Combo (#616)
It's a table, a bench, and a chaise lounge. Easy-to-build. **$2.00**

E. Patio Cover (#560)
Built from plastic panels. Size can be altered. **$2.00**

G. Robot Chest (#706)
48" high x 22" wide x 16" deep, holds lots of clothes and toys.

H. Froggy High Chair (#525)
3½' high. Trace pattern onto plywood, saw and paint. **$2.00**

I. Cooking/Serving Carts (#543)
Also a portable bar. Step-by-step photos. **$2.00**

J. Ferns From Mother Nature (#H501)
Handy hints for growing beautiful ferns. **$3.50**

A. Playhouse (#418)
Style is A-Frame. **$1.00**

B. Cat Cabin (#442)
Enter from front or side **$1.50**

C. Pony (#387)
Sturdy & safe. **$1.00**

D. Playhouse (#332)
Collapsible. **$1.50**

E. Locomotive (#458)
Steers with ease.

F. Child's Glider (#445)
Trace-cut-paint. **$1.50**

G. Playhouse (#224)
Kids love it! **$1.50**

H. Sand Box (#164)
Or wading pool. **$1.50**

I. Monkey Gym (#159)
Safe & durable. **$1.50**

J. Fort Apache (#635)
4' x 4' playhouse. **$2.00**

K. Toy Box (#630)
18" w x 34" l x 18" h. **$2.00**

L. Patio Table (#313)
Just for kids! **$1.00**

M. Colonial Cradle (#87)
Or planter box. **$1.00**

N. Desk & Seat (#74)
Child-size. **$1.00**

O. Dining Buffet (#576)
2'x30" folded up. **$2.50**

P. Dutch Buffet (#583)
71"h x 50"w x 20"d. **$2.50**

107

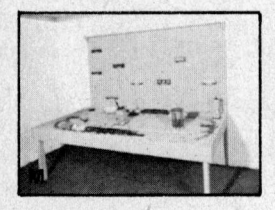

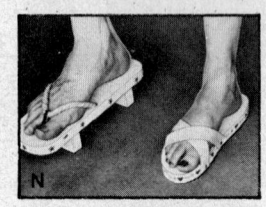

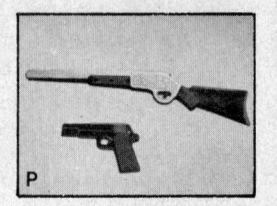

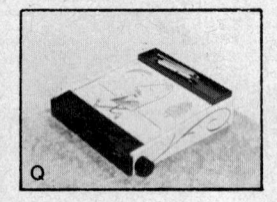

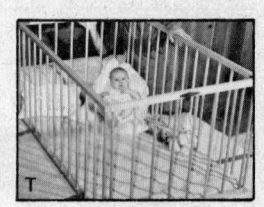

A. Bookends (#73)
Horseheads. $1.00

B. Toy Chest (#137)
Pulls easily. $1.00

C. Wheelbarrow (#59)
Easy-to-do. $1.00

D. Playhouse (#309)
Fort/toolshed. $1.00

E. Teeter-Totter (#100)
Fun for kids! $1.00

F. Cat Bunk Bed (#465)
Sandbox hidden. $2.00

G. Traffic Signs (#520)
Cut & paint. $1.00

H. Kiddy Diesel (#627)
Full-size pattern.

I. Pull Toys (#1)
4 animals. $2.00

J. Dog House (#136)
Simple-to-do. $1.00

K. Pet Bunk (#170)
Dog or cat. $1.00

L. Pet Dinette (#89)
A snap! $1.00

M. Train Table (#362)
Slot cars too! $1.00

N. Wooden Shoes (#90)
Good for feet! $1.00

O. Step Chair (#102)
Need a lift? $1.00

P. Toy Guns (#150)
Set of two. $1.00

Q. Scribble Box (#212)
Child's desk. $1.00

R. Playhouse (#549)
Shoe-style! $2.00

S. Kiddie Toter (#401)
Sling-style. $1.00

T. Play Pen (#196)
Folds up. $1.00

A. Pet Seat (#540)
Also pet door. $1.50

B. Bike Rack (#457)
Fits car top. $1.00

C. Luggage Rack (#228)
Rain-proof. $1.00

D. Car-Kitchen (#406)
Fits on car. $1.00

E. Trailer (#449)
Easy-travel. $2.00

F. Swimming Pools (#471)
Eleven different shapes.

G. Camper (#526)
Pop-up style. $2.00

H. Car-Camper (#281)
Room for 2. $1.50

I. Picnic Basket (#433)
Carries all! $1.00

J. Tackle Box (#200)
Pull-tray. $1.00

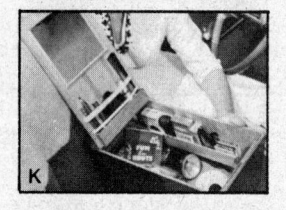

K. Travel Aid (#201)
Handy case. $1.00

L. Tackle Box (#421)
Lures, etc. $1.00

M. Kitchen Case (#479)
Holds pots. $1.00

N. Camp Diner (#336)
Seats 6. $2.00

O. Paddle Duck (#440)
Pedal it! $1.50

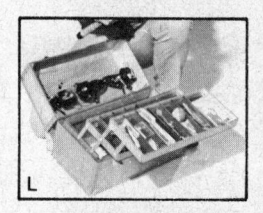

P. Scooter (#428)
Water-safe. $1.50

Q. Plyak (#504)
11 ft. $2.00

R. Sailboard (#450)
10 ft. $1.50

S. House Boat (#469)
Fun & sun! $2.00

T. Skimmer (#472)
Carries 2. $1.50

109

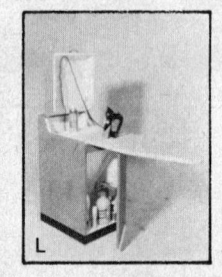

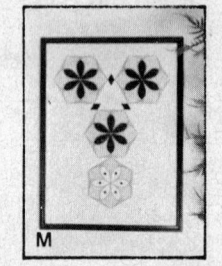

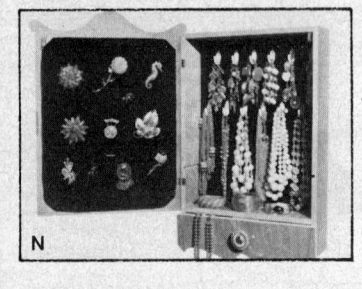

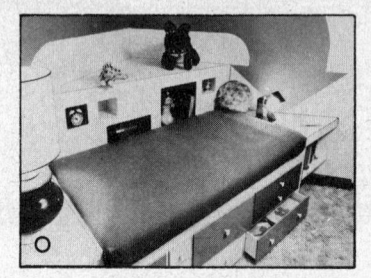

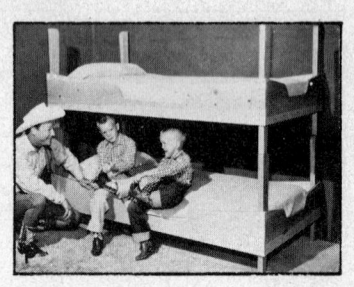

A. **Round Card Table (#431)**
Seats 8. $1.50

B. **Bridge Table (#305)**
Contoured to fit. $1.50

C. **Butler's Cart (#364)**
3 trays. $1.00

D. **Picture Bar (#223)**
Den or office. $1.00

E. **Dough Box (#280)**
Colonial-style. $1.50

F. **Hall Vanity (#403)**
Mirror & drawer. $1.00

G. **Lectern/Bookcase (#376)**
On casters.

H. **3-D String Art (#HA31)**
7 designs in all. $2.00

I. **Lamp Post (#353)**
Easy-to-do $1.00

J. **Shopping Cart (#94)**
Handy item! $1.00

K. **Back Rest (#236)**
Folds up. $1.00

L. **Ironing Center (#349)**
Fold-up cabinet. $1.50

M. **Flower Picture (#490)**
Yarn and tacks. $1.00

N. **Jewel Cabinet (#389)**
Elegant. $1.00

O. **Altogether Bed (#565)**
Great for a corner. $2.00

P. **Bunk Beds (#134)**
Space saver. $1.00

LETTERS

"Please make your patterns known all over so that people like ourselves can use them to make their children gifts." (refers to small boy's jeep)
Mrs. Harold Coates
Las Vegas, Nevada

"I built your double chaise lounge and it's the envy of the neighborhood."
W. Lynn Nelson
Vernal, Utah

"Thank you so much for making us amateurs look so good in woodworking."
Charles Glotta
Wichita, Kansas

"I have purchased patterns from you before... good results every time."
D. G. LaPointe
Long Beach, Calif.

"I find your patterns best from all others I have tried."
Henry W. Lavalley
Dalton, Mass.

"Never could pound a nail straight without hitting my fingers but with your string owl project I really had fun."
Mrs. O. C. Jenkins
Washington, Ohio

111

$3.00...All Pattern Prices are $3.00 Unless Marked Otherwise
(plus postage)

Postage & Handling Charges

Total Amount of Order	1st Class
Up to $3.00	1.00
3.01 to 5.00	1.50
5.01 to 7.50	2.00
7.51 to 10.00	2.50

Over $10.00 add: 25% for 1st class
California residents please add 6% sales tax.

All Canadian orders must be accompanied by U.S. funds. No Airmail shipments to Canada. Sorry – we cannot ship to any other foreign country.

NOTE: There is sometimes a delay in delivery due to unusually heavy orders. If you have also ordered a catalog, it will arrive after the patterns. Please allow 4-6 weeks for your completed order to arrive.

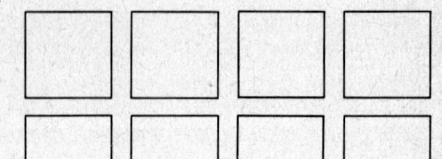

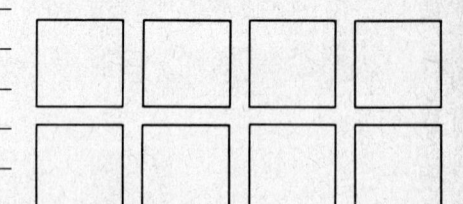

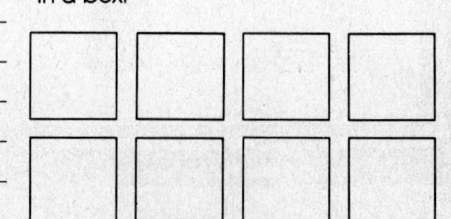

U bild
8088
Box 2383
Van Nuys, CA 91409

TOTAL OF ORDER $ _____
LESS 10% DISCOUNT $ _____
(orders of $10 or more)
SUB-TOTAL $ _____
PLUS POSTAGE & HANDLING $ _____
(See chart)
TOTAL AMOUNT: $ _____
NAME _____
ADDRESS _____
CITY _____
STATE _____ ZIP _____

Please print name and address and enclose check or money order for your pattern selection.

Place each pattern or book number in a box.

[ ] [ ] [ ] [ ]
[ ] [ ] [ ] [ ]

Check here for $1.95 catalog ☐

U bild
8088
Box 2383
Van Nuys, CA 91409

TOTAL OF ORDER $ _____
LESS 10% DISCOUNT $ _____
(orders of $10 or more)
SUB-TOTAL $ _____
PLUS POSTAGE & HANDLING $ _____
(See chart)
TOTAL AMOUNT: $ _____
NAME _____
ADDRESS _____
CITY _____
STATE _____ ZIP _____

Please print name and address and enclose check or money order for your pattern selection.

Place each pattern or book number in a box.

[ ] [ ] [ ] [ ]
[ ] [ ] [ ] [ ]

Check here for $1.95 catalog ☐

U bild
8088
Box 2383
Van Nuys, CA 91409

TOTAL OF ORDER $ _____
LESS 10% DISCOUNT $ _____
(orders of $10 or more)
SUB-TOTAL $ _____
PLUS POSTAGE & HANDLING $ _____
(See chart)
TOTAL AMOUNT: $ _____
NAME _____
ADDRESS _____
CITY _____
STATE _____ ZIP _____

Please print name and address and enclose check or money order for your pattern selection.

Place each pattern or book number in a box.

[ ] [ ] [ ] [ ]
[ ] [ ] [ ] [ ]

Check here for $1.95 catalog ☐